Ultimate Paranormal
Guide

ULTIMATE PARANORMAL GUIDE

Printed in the United States.

ISBN-13: 978-1494781910
ISBN-10: 1494781913

ULTIMATE PARANORMAL GUIDE

TABLE OF CONTENTS

**Paranormal • Spectrological • UFOlogy
Cryptozoology • Belief • Education
Science • Mythology • Folklore**

ULTIMATE PARANORMAL GUIDE

A

Aboriginal: Pagan tradition of the native Australian people.

Abducted: A human or an animal that has been captured. The act of taking a person against their will.

Abominable Snowman: (Cryptozoology) See Yeti.

Adept: An individual who through serious study and accomplishments is considered highly proficient in a particular magickal system.

Active: Ongoing reported claims of a haunting or unexplained paranormal phenomenon.

Adamski, George: George, who ran a café near the Mount Palomar Observatory, was the most famous of the contactees of the early fifties. In his book Flying Saucers Have Landed, he claimed to have met aliens from Venus. This was before scientists learned that Venus has a surface temperature of around 900 degrees. He later claimed to been taken aboard a flying saucer for a tour of the solar system.

AFOSI: The Air Force Office of Special Investigations. A sort of Air Force version of the FBI. It said to have been involved in UFO investigations many times.

Afterlife: Almost every society and religion has some belief in life after death. The Christian version of the afterlife involves some type of judgment upon the body's demise and the assignment of the soul to either Heaven or Hell, while many societies believe that life simply continues in another plane of existence.

Agent: The apparition, or ghost, seen by a human being (or percipient).

Airships: In 1896 & 1897, there was a wave of sightings across the United States of propeller-driven aircraft similar to dirigibles, although lighter than air balloons have been around since 1785. The reports are regarded as a series of newspaper hoaxes and "Liar's Club" tales.

Akasha Spirit: The fifth element, the omnipresent spiritual power that permeates the universe.

Alchemy: A branch of High Magick developed in the middle Ages, which sought to magickally and/or chemically turn base metals into gold.

Alien: (UFOlogy) A being from another planet. An extraterrestrial. There are many types mentioned, including Grays: Small humanoids with large heads and large eyes, Reptoids: Described as a reptilian creature. Nordics: Blond, blue-eyed humanoids. Oddly, the types of aliens reported vary from country to country. European reports favor dwarves, and South

American reports often mention hairy dwarves, while Americans usually see Grays or Nordics, with occasional Reptoids.

Alien Greys: Was the first of three types of aliens that are being held in custody by the U.S. government at Area 51.

Alien Abduction: Some people, including writer Whitley Strieber, have had experiences in which they were taken from their beds or cars by aliens who took them into their craft for medical tests and other things. Sometimes the people involved remember these experiences, but sometimes they only recall them after being hypnotized. There is much disagreement as to whether these experiences are real or whether they are some type of dreamlike phenomenon.

Allagash Abductions: Four men were abducted in 1976 while fishing on the Allagash waterway in Maine. Also a book by Raymond Fowler.

Allende Carlos (AKA Carl Allen): Merchant Marine sailor on the S. S. Andrew Furuseth who later wrote letters to Morris K. Jessup, author of The Case for the UFO. In those letters, he claimed to have been a witness to the Philadelphia Experiment.

Altar: A special, flat surface set aside exclusively for magickal workings or religious acknowledgment.

Alternating current (AC): The flow of electric charge periodically reverses direction.

Alternative 3: TV program and book about a group of the "elite" leaving earth for colonies on the Moon and Mars.

Amulet: A magically charged object, which deflects specific, usually negative energies. A protective object.

Ancient Astronauts: Some people, such as Erich von Daniken, claim that archaeological evidence proves that aliens visited Earth in the past. Some also claim to find evidence of such visitation in the religions and mythology of various cultures. Zecharia Sitchin is one of these. Mainstream archaeologists generally find these ideas to be amusing cocktail party chatter.

Angel: A supernatural being that exists on the level between God and mortals is said to be an angel. One of the duties of the angels is thought to act as guardians over humans.

Angel Hair: long, thin wispy fibers that been seen to fall from the sky after some UFO sightings. It has been very difficult to collect samples for analysis because angel hair disintegrates quickly. One theory about angel hair is that is actually the web of certain types of spiders that travel about on the wind, using webbing like a parachute or hang glider.

Ankh: An Egyptian hieroglyphic widely used as a symbol of life, love, and reincarnation. It is a cross with a looped top.

Annunaki: Ancient astronauts posited by Zecheriah Sitchin based on his interpretation of ancient Sumerian texts.

Both has minor variations in meaning which has to do with more the characteristics, and properties of the anomaly. See Electronic Voice Phenomenon (EVP)

Anomalous Voice Phenomenon (AVP)
Anomalous: Is more accepted in mainstream science.

Acoustical Voice Phenomenon (AVP)

Anomalistic Psychology: The scientific study of anomalous phenomena, including, but not limited to, such parapsychological events as ESP, life-after-death experiences and alleged alien abduction experiences.

Anomaly: A strange occurrence that cannot be rationalized by objective critical scientific evaluation.

Anpsi: Referring to psi ability in non-human animals; a contraction of "animal PSI." See PSI.

Anthropology: Is the study of humans, past and present. To understand the complexity of cultures across all of human history.

Anthropomorphism is any attribution of human characteristics (or characteristics assumed to belong only to humans) to animals, non-living things, phenomena, material states, objects or abstract concepts, such as spirits or deities. The term coined in the mid-1700s. Examples include animals, plants, and forces of nature such as winds, rain or the sun depicted as creatures with human motivations, and/or the abilities to reason and converse.

Anubis: God of mummification in Egypt.

Aphrodite: (Mythology) the Greek goddess of love, beauty, pleasure, and procreation. She is the daughter of Zeus and Dione.

Apollo: (Mythology) a god of light and the sun, truth and prophecy, healing, plague, music, poetry, and more. Apollo is the son of Zeus and Leto, and has a twin sister, the chaste huntress Artemis.

Apophenia: is the experience of seeing meaningful patterns or connections in random or meaningless data.

Apport/Asport: An apport is a solid object that seemingly appears from nowhere in the presence of a medium. Some apports are assembled from invisible material matter; others are teleported from another often-distant location. An asport is any object that spirits or the medium makes disappear or teleports to another location.

Apparition: See Ghost.

APRO: Aerial Phenomena Research Organization - A UFO group founded in 1952 by Coral and Jim Lorenzen. For most of its existence, it was based in Tucson, Arizona. Jim passed away in1986, and Coral in 1988 and APRO passed with them.

Arcana: The two halves of a tarot deck. The Major Arcana consists of 22 trumps, the Minor Arcana consists of 56 suit cards (sometimes called the lesser or lower Arcana).

Area 51: "Area 51" is a super-secret Air Force Base located on the Nevada Test Range. It has several other names, including Groom Lake. The name "Area 51" came from the fact that the site was labeled as "Area 51" on old Atomic Energy Commission maps. The name "Groom Lake" comes from the fact that the base's runway, the longest runway in the world, is located in a dry lakebed named Groom Lake. This secret base is used for testing top-secret black budget aircraft. It has been rumored that there are captured alien craft being tested there also.

Ares: (Mythology) is the Greek god of war. He represents the physical or violent and untamed aspect of war, in contrast to the armored Athena, whose functions as a goddess of intelligence include military strategy and generalship. The son of Zeus and Hera.

Argus: (Mythology) a giant with 100 eyes; was guardian of the heifer Io and was slain by Hermes.

Arnold, Kenneth: While flying over the Cascade Mountains in Washington State on June 24, 1947, businessman/pilot Kenneth Arnold observed nine heel-shaped craft that he described as moving like a "saucer skipping over water". Thus was born the term flying saucer.

Artemis: (Mythology) the Hellenic goddess of the hunt, wild animals, wilderness, childbirth, virginity and protector of young girls, bringing and relieving disease in women; she often was depicted as a huntress carrying a bow and arrows.

Asimov, Isaac (January 2, 1920 - April 6, 1992) Born in Petrovichi, Russia, Isaac Asimov immigrated with his family to the United States and became a biochemistry professor while pursuing writing. He published his first novel, Pebble in the Sky, in 1950. An immensely prolific author who penned nearly 500 books, he published influential sci-fi works like I, Robot and the Foundation trilogy, as well as books in a variety of other genres. Asimov died in New York City from heart and kidney failure related to AIDS.

Aspect: The particular principle or part of the Creative Life Force being worked with or acknowledged at any one time.

Asperger: A bundle of fresh herbs or a perforated object used to sprinkle water during or preceding ritual, for purification purposes.

Astral Plane: A world that believed to exist above our physical world.

Astral Plane: A place, generally conceptualized as an invisible parallel world, which remains unseen from our own solid world of form.

Astral Body: One's soul, appearing as an exact double of the person's physical body, separated temporarily as during a dream or out-of-body experience or permanently as in death.
See doppelganger.

Astral Projection: The process of separating your astral body from your physical one to accomplish travel in the astral plane or dream time. Also, see Out-of-body experience.

Astrology: The study of and belief in the effects the movements and placements of planets and other heavenly bodies have on the lives and behavior of human beings.

Astronaut UFO Sightings: Since the advent of the U.S. space program, there have been rumors that our astronauts have seen UFOs while in space.

Athame: A cleansed and consecrated ritual blade. Usually double-edged and black handled. It is never used to cut anything on the physical plane. Pronounced several ways: Ah-THAM-ee ATH-ah-may ah-THAW-may.

Athena: (Mythology) the goddess of wisdom, courage, inspiration, civilization, law and justice, just warfare, mathematics, strength, strategy, the arts, crafts, and skill. Another daughter of Zeus.

Audio Pareidolia: see Pareidolia

Aura: Refers to the energy field emanating from the surface of a person or object. This emanation visualized as an outline of cascading color, and may be held to represent soul vibrations, chakra emergence, or a reflection of surrounding energy fields.

Automatic Writing: Form of divination where the channeler uses a pen, paper and an altered state of consciousness to receive messages

Automatic Writing: Communication from a spirit in written form. The medium holds a pen or pencil against paper and allows the spirit to take possession or control of his or her hand to write out a message.

Automatism: Any unconscious and spontaneous muscular movement caused by the spirits. Automatic writing and sleepwalking are forms of automatism.

Autonographist Professional: automatic writer.

Aviary: Collective name for a loosely knit group of "contacts" in the government and military who were involved with UFOs and who were given bird code names by William L. Moore.

Aztec, New Mexico: Site of a supposed UFO crash in 1948.

ULTIMATE PARANORMAL GUIDE

B

Balefire: A fire lit for magickal purposes, usually outdoors. They are traditional on Yule, Beltane, and Midsummer.

Ball Lightning: An unexplained atmospheric electrical phenomenon, little understood and very rare form of lightning. Some scientists doubt its existence because all of the evidence is anecdotal. The descriptions most often given are that it is spherical, short-lived, usually only a few centimeters in diameter, and is seen accompanying ordinary lightning. Some to explain UFO sightings, although it fits very few sighting descriptions, have used it.

Ball Plasma: see Ball Lightning.

Bane: That which destroys life, which is poisonous, destructive, dangerous.

Banish-(ment): The expulsion of a ghost, spirit, demon, or other entity/entities thought to be possessing, haunting a human being or location. The ritual, is usually secular in nature, but may call upon some Higher Power to cast out the evil force(s). See Exorcism.

Banshee: A female death omen spirit of Ireland and Scotland that attaches itself to families especially those whose surnames begin with "Mac" and "O" and manifests to herald an approaching death in the family. See Doppelgänger.

Basilisk: (Mythology) a mythical snake-like creature reputed to be so venomous its gaze was deadly.

B.C.E.: Before Common Era. Synonymous with B.C. without religious bias.

Bells: (Belief) often used as ritual tools. They can be used to invoke directional energies, to ring in the sunrise on a Sabbat, or to frighten away faeries and baneful spirits.

Besom: A witch's broom.

Bermuda Triangle (The Devil's Triangle): Is one of the two places on earth that a magnetic compass does point towards true north. Normally it points toward magnetic north. The difference between the two is known as compass variation. The modern Bermuda Triangle legend did not get started until 1950 when the Associated Press published an article written by Edward Van Winkle Jones. Jones reported several incidences of disappearing ships and planes in the Bermuda Triangle, including five US Navy torpedo bombers that vanished on December 5, 1945, and the commercial airliners "Star Tiger" and "Star Ariel" which disappeared on January 30, 1948 and January 17, 1949 respectively. All told, about 135 individuals were unaccounted for, and they all went missing around the Bermuda Triangle.

It was a 1955 book, The Case for the UFO, by M. K. Jessup that started pointing fingers at alien life forms. After all, no bodies or wreckage had yet been discovered. By 1964, Vincent H. Gaddis who coined the term "Bermuda Triangle."

The Bermuda Triangle obsession hit its peak in the early 1970s with the publication of several paperback books about the topic, including the bestseller by Charles Berlitz, The Bermuda Triangle.

Larry Kusche, who published The Bermuda Triangle Mystery: Solved in 1975, argued that other authors had exaggerated their numbers and had not done any proper research.

Belgian UFO Sightings: Eupen & Wavre, Belgium were the site of a series of mysterious UFO sightings in 1989 - 1990.

Bennewitz, Paul: An Albuquerque, New Mexico physicist and electronics firm owner. He was also a member of the APRO UFO group, and in 1979, he began monitoring strange lights over the Manzano Test Range Facility. Originator of the Dulce base story.

Bentwaters-Woodbridge: Forest near Woodbridge, Suffolk, England. It was the site of a well-known UFO event on 27 December 1980. Also known as the Rendlesham Forest UFO event.

Bloody Mary: (Folklore) A witch that was burn to death, as she burned she screamed a curse. If anyone mentioned her name aloud before a mirror, she would send her spirit to revenge herself upon him or her for her terrible death. To chant Bloody Mary's name three times before a darkened mirror will summon the vengeful spirit of the witch.

Boianai, Papua, New Guinea: Anglican missionary Father William Booth Gill reported UFOs over Boianai, Papua, New Guinea in 1959.

Brazel, William "Mac": Sheep rancher who first discovered the Roswell debris on the Foster Ranch in 1947.

Brown Lady of Raynham Hall is a picture of the spirit of Lady Townshend taken on December 16, 1936, by photographers from Country Life magazine. "Brown Lady" so named because of the brown brocade dress that she wears. The photo analyst Joe Nickell examined the photograph and concluded that it was nothing more than two images composited together.

Browne, Sylvia: Born Sylvia Celeste Shoemaker (October 19, 1936, November 20, 2013) alleged

Psychic Medium. She author dozens of books and publications, some including topics of the afterlife for both humans and pets, dreams, healing, end of the world predictions and prophecies, and "Angels, Guides and Ghosts. Was a frequent TV guest psychic on "The Montel Williams Show."

Bigfoot: See Yeti.

Bigelow, Robert (born 1945) is an American hotel and aerospace entrepreneur. He owns the hotel chain Budget Suites of America and is the founder of Bigelow Aerospace and founded National Institute for Discovery Science. Before becoming president and founder of the National Institute for Discovery Science, Robert was a long-time financer into "research" of such topics as dreams, meditation, hypnosis, out-of-body experiences, telepathy, and the ever-popular subject among college students, drug-induced altered states of consciousness.

Bi-Location: A type of astral projection during which you maintain awareness of your present surroundings.

Bind: (Witchcraft) to magickally, restrain something or someone.

Bioelectromagnetism: (sometimes equated with bioelectricity) refers to the electrical, magnetic or electromagnetic fields produced by living cells, tissues or organisms. Examples include the cell membrane potential and the electric currents that flow in nerves and muscles, because of action potentials.

Biofield: See Bioelectromagnetism

Black Aircraft: Experimental top-secret aircraft whose development paid for out of the black budget. The U-2 spy plane, the SR-71 Blackbird, and the Stealth Fighter all began as "Black Aircraft." Many of these aircraft tested at Area 51.just north of Las Vegas Nevada

Black Budget: A "slush fund" of federal budget money that can be spent without specific justification to Congress. This is possible because it is deemed necessary for defense research in order to maintain National Security.

Black Magick: Traditionally referred to the use of supernatural powers or magic for evil and selfish purposes. With respect to the philosophy of left-hand path and right-hand path, black magic is the malicious counterpart of benevolent white magick.

Blood of the Moon: A woman's menstrual cycle. Should this cycle occur over a Full Moon or New Moon, she is far more powerful than during any other time of the month, as long as she acknowledges this strength within herself.

Blue Book, Project: The third, and longest lasting, Air Force UFO investigation. Its main objective was to explain [away] UFO reports.

Blue Lady: The ghost of a woman reportedly seen in and around the Moss Beach Distillery Cafe in Moss Beach, California; she is so-named because she usually dressed all in blue. Although later disproven after episode 411 of Ghost Hunters as a hoax perpetrated by the staff.

Bokors: In the religion of vodou are sorcerers or houngan (priests) or mambo (priestesses) for hire who are said to 'serve the loa with both hands', meaning that they practice both dark magick and white magick. Their black magick includes the creation of zombies and the creation of 'ouangas', talismans that house spirits.

Boline: A white-handled knife, used in magick and ritual for purposes such as cutting herbs or piercing a pomegranate.

Boogeyman: (bogeyman) Referring to a monster whose name is invoked by parents or other adults to frighten children into obedience.

Book of Shadows: A witch's book of spells, rituals, magickal lore. Much akin to a magickal cookbook. Also known as a BOS.

Burning Times: Reference to a historical time from around 1000 C.E. through the 17th century when it is said that up to nine million people were tortured and burned by church and public officials on the assumption that they were the Christian version of Witches. This turned into an extremely profitable venture, as all land and property was seized from the accused individual and portions given to the accuser (in reward fashion) and the remainder seized by the church officials. Historians indicate that the majority of people tortured and murdered were women and children as young as the age of 2 years old.

C

Calibration: Is a comparison between measurements one of known magnitude or correctness made or set with one device and another measurement made in as similar a way as possible with a second device.

Recalibration Mel-8704 EMF meter

Step one
Hold REC/ENTER and HOLD/ESCAPE buttons down at the same time. Turn the meter on while you continue to hold the above buttons down. When the meter turns on S-ON will appear.

Step two
Release the buttons and zero will appear, quickly press the up button until 9 appears and press enter.

The number 100 will show up and the numbers above it will move allow 5 seconds for the numbers to stabilize and press enter. 200 will show up allow 5 seconds for the numbers to stabilize and press enter. 300 will show up allow 5 seconds for the numbers to stabilize and press enter. Turn the meter off. Now turn the meter on. 0.0 should displayed if the calibration was good.

Call: Invoking Divine forces.

Calling Ghosts: Spirits who call out the names of the living in order to lure them to their deaths are called calling ghosts. The sirens of Greek mythology were calling ghosts.

Cardoso, Anabela is a philologist and a career diplomat. Her involvement in ITC experimentation was the result of unexpected circumstances. Her positive results drove her to set aside her professional life and devote full time to this fascinating field of research. She is the founder and the Editor of the ITC Journal. She has published articles and given presentations on ITC worldwide. She recently completed an important project of investigation designed to record anomalous electronic voices under controlled conditions. A Two-Year Study of Allegedly Anomalous Electronic Voices or EVP published in NeuroQuantology 2012; (3: 492-514) Controlled experiments aimed at the recording of the purportedly anomalous electronic voices (EVP) were carried out in Vigo, Spain, during the years 2008 and 2009. Dr. Anabela Cardoso (2010) was the research project director and the main operator of the EVP tests.

Case Study: (Science) An in-depth investigation of an individual subject.

Cash: (Landrum Incident) In 1980, near Huffman, Texas, Betty Cash, Vickie Landrum, and Betty's grandson Colby had a close encounter with a UFO that was apparently being escorted by military helicopters.

The three, particularly Betty Cash, then had a series of health problems that they felt were related to their encounter.

Caul: A thin membrane of amniotic fluid that remains covering the head of a newborn at birth. Those born with a caul are said to be blessed with luck, protection and supernatural powers. Such individuals are thought to be able to see and speak with ghosts and spirits.

C.E.: Common Era. Synonymous with A.D. but without religious bias.

Censer: A heatproof container in which incense is burned. It is associated with the element air.

Cerberus: (Greek mythology) Hellhound the three-headed dog guarding the entrance to Hades; son of Typhon.

Ceremonial Magick: A highly codified magickal tradition based upon Kabbalah, the Jewish-Gnostic mystical teachings.

Cattle Mutilations: Ranchers find cattle dead, with soft body parts such as eyes, lips, udders, and sex organs surgically removed. Whodunit? Sometimes UFOs are seen concurrently with the mutilations, and sometimes-black helicopters are seen in the area.

Cauldron: Linked to witchcraft in the popular mind, this symbolizes the Goddess, the waters of rebirth.

Chakras: Seven major energy vortexes found in the human body. Each is usually associated with a color. They are: crown - white; third eye - purple; throat - blue; chest - pink or green; navel - yellow; abdomen - orange groin - red. Smaller vortexes are located in the hands and feet as well.

Chalcedony: A type of translucent quartz, usually a smoky blue in color, which was used by the ancient Egyptians to drive away ghosts, night visions and sadness.

Chalice: A ritual tool. It represents the female principals of creation.

Channeling: A New Age practice wherein you allow a discarnate entity to "borrow" your body to speak to others either through automatic writing or verbally.

Chaplet: A crown for the head usually made of flowers and worn at Beltane.

Charon: (Greek mythology) the ferryman who brought the souls of the dead across the river Styx or the river Acheron to Hades.

Charge: The Originally written in modern form by Doreen Valiente, it is a story of the message from Goddess to Her children.

Charging: To infuse an object with personal power.

Charms: Either an amulet or talisman that has been charmed by saying an incantation over it and instilling it with energy for a specific task.

Chiles, Clarence: Eastern Airlines pilot who sighted a UFO near Montgomery, Alabama, on July 24, 1948.

China: A wave of UFO sightings occurred in China at the end of 1999.

Chupacabra: (Spanish pronunciation "goat sucker") Part legend and rumor the animal inhabit parts of the Americas, with the first sightings reported in Puerto Rico. The name comes from the animal's reported habit of attacking and drinking the blood of livestock, especially goats.

Cigar: UFOs reported to be cigar-shaped.

Circle: Sacred space wherein all magick is to be worked and all ritual contained. It both holds ritual energy until the witch is ready to release it, and provides protection for the witch.

Clairalience: The ability to receive a spirit's message through smell.

Clairambience: The ability to receive a spirit's message through taste.

Clairaudience: The ability to receive a spirit's message through sound.

Clairsentience: The ability to feel or sense a spirit's presence and/or message.

Clairvoyance: A type of extrasensory perception (ESP), clairvoyance is the ability to see objects, events, places and people not visible through normal sight. Some individuals gifted with clairvoyance throughout their lives while others may experience only one clairvoyant event in their life.

Cleansing: Removing negative energies from an object or space.

Close Encounters: See Hynek UFO Classification System.

Collective Unconsciousness: Term used to describe the sentient connection of all living things, past and present. See also Akashic Records.

Collective Apparition: An unusual type of spirit sighting in which more than one person sees the same apparition.

Collective Unconscious: The analytical psychology of Carl Jung, the collective unconscious is the collective memory of all of humanity's past, held in an individual's unconscious mind.

Coming of Age Ritual: At age 13 for boys, and at the time of a girl's first menses, Pagan children are seen as spiritual adults. The ritual celebrates their new maturity. Generally, this is the age when they are permitted membership in covens.

Condon Report: In 1966, the US Air Force commissioned the University of Colorado to make a scientific study of UFOs. Headed by Dr. Edward Condon, in 1969 the group published The Scientific Study of Unidentified Flying Objects, which debunked the UFO phenomena. The Condon Report was used as an excuse to close down Project Blue Book, which many say was its only purpose anyhow.

Cone of Power: Psychic energy raised and focused by either an individual or a group mind (coven) to achieve a definite purpose.

Confabulation: A term used to describe when real-life experiences are mixed with imagined ones.

Conscious Mind: The analytical, materially based, rational half of our consciousness. The part of our mind that is at work while we balance our checkbooks, theorize, communicate, and perform other acts related to the physical world.

Consecration: The act of blessing an object or place by instilling it with positive energy.

Contactee: A person who claims that aliens have visited him personally.

Control: This is a procedure in paranormal psychology that ensures that the experiment is conducted in a standard fashion so that the results will not be influenced by any extraneous factors.

Control Group: A group of outside subjects whose performance or abilities are compared with the experimental subjects.

Cooper, Milton William "Bill": Radio personality and writer of Behold a Pale Horse. Noted for various conspiracy theories.

Corona: A type of plasma "atmosphere" of the Sun or other celestial body, extending millions of kilometers into space, most easily seen during a total solar eclipse, but also observable in a coronagraph. The Latin root of the word corona means crown.

Corso, Colonel Philip J. Retired U.S. Army, author of *The Day after Roswell*. Claimed in the book, to have been given technology from the crashed Roswell UFO for the purpose of leaking the technology surreptitiously to American industry and the military.

Coven: A group of thirteen or fewer witches that work together in an organized fashion for positive magickal endeavors or to perform religious ceremonies.

Coven stead: The meeting place of witches, often a fixed building or place where the witch can feel safe and at home.

Coyne, Captain Lawrence J. Coyne & others aboard a National Guard helicopter had a close brush with a UFO in 1973 near Mansfield, Ohio.

Craft: see Witchcraft.

Crisis Apparition: An apparition that is seen when a person is seriously ill, seriously injured or at the point of death.

Crop Circles: In the 1970s, large, circles of flattened grain began to appear in British fields. The circles gradually became more complex, forming something like pictograms. Many researchers tried to explain them by theories including magnetic fields, plasma vortices, twisters, alien visitors leaving messages, and love crazed hedgehogs. In 1991, two people named Doug

37

Bower and Dave Chorley of Southampton in Britain announced that they had been making crop circles for 15 years. They had hatched the idea over a pint or two in their local pub. No matter. The circles continue to appear, and have spread all over the world.

Crone: Aspect of the Goddess represented by the old woman. Symbolized by the waning moon, the carrion crow, the cauldron, the color black. Her Sabbats are Mabon and Sambaing.

Cross Correspondences: Interrelated bits of information received from the spirit world by different mediums at different times and locations. The communications must be joined together to form a complete message from the spirit(s).

Cross-Quarter Days: Refers to Sabbat not falling on the solstices or equinoxes.

Cryptozoology: The study of hidden animals; the search for animals whose existence has not been proven.

Cryptozoologist: A specialist studying in the field of Cryptozoology.

Crystal Skulls: Allegedly said to of been mention in many tribal indigenous communities in North America, the Mayans, the Incans and even Tibetan Himalayan shamanism. The British Museum established that it is not an authentic pre-Columbian artefact and made with modern tools from a block of clear quartz around 19th century AD. The scientific community claim that there is no evidence of any unusual phenomena associated with the skulls.

CUFOS: Center for UFO Studies - Group founded by Astronomer J. Allen Hynek in 1973.

Cyclops Shark (Cryptozoology) has a single, functioning eye at the front of its head the hallmark of a congenital condition called cyclopia, which occurs in several animal species, including humans.

D

Daimon: (Greek Mythology) See Demon.

Days of Power: They can also be days triggered by astrological occurrences such as your birthday, a woman's menstrual cycle, your dedication/initiation anniversary. See Sabbat.

Decibel originates from methods used to quantify reductions in audio levels in telephone circuits. These losses originally measured in units of Miles of Standard Cable seldom-used unit named in honor of Alexander Graham Bell.

dB is not based on a unit of measurement but a scale of amplitude.

dBm power of sound in watts = 0.001 (one mill watt)

Debunker: A person who attempts to expose or discredit claims believed to be false, exaggerated or pretentious. The term is closely associated with skeptical investigation of controversial topics such as UFO, Bigfoot, and Ghosts.

Dedication: The process where an individual accepts the Craft as their path and vows to study and learn all that is necessary to reach adept-ship. It is a conscious preparation to accept something new into your life and stick with it, regardless of the highs and lows that may follow.

Déjà vu: French for "already seen;" the feeling or illusion of having previously experienced an event or place actually being encountered for the first time.

Delphos, Kansas: Site where the Johnson family had a close encounter in 1971.

Demeter: (Mythology) is the goddess of the harvest, who presided over grains and the fertility of the earth. Her cult titles include Sito (wheat) as the giver of food or corn/grain and Thesmophoros (divine order, un-written law) as a mark of the civilized existence of agricultural society.

Demigod: A divine or supernatural being in classical mythology. The term has been used in various ways at different times and can refer to a figure who has attained divine status after death, a minor deity, or a mortal who is the offspring of a god and a human.

Demon: An evil or satanic spirit; a devil; a wicked, cruel, persistently tormenting being or person tending to cause harm.

Demonology: (Paranormal) The study of evil spirits.

Deosil: Clockwise, the direction in which the shadow on a sundial moves as the Sun "moves" across the sky. Symbolic of life, positive magick, and positive energies.

Devil: The personified spirit of evil; ruler of Hell, and enemy of God. Also, see Demon.

Devil's Triangle: Another name for the Bermuda Triangle.

Dionysus: (Mythology) the god of the grape harvest, winemaking and wine, of ritual madness and ecstasy in Greek mythology. He was the youngest and the only one to have a mortal mother.

Direct current (DC): The electric current flows in a constant direction.

Direct Voice Phenomenon (DVP): A spirit voice, spoken directly to sitters at a séance. The sound usually seems to come from a point near the medium, or through a spirit horn or trumpet, but not from the mouth of the medium.

Direct Writing: A spectral phenomenon, seen most often in a séance, in which spirit handwriting appears directly on a previously unmarked surface.

Dirk: Ritual knife of the Scottish tradition.

Discarnate Entity: See ghost.

Disembodied Voices: When a person witnesses the inexplicable sound of voices although it is quite clear that no one is present at the time

Disinformation: An intelligence tactic used to protect top-secret information by diluting or covering the truth with false information.

Divination: The act of acquiring information via paranormal means, such as via tarot cards, palmistry, scrying, etc.

Divination: The magickal art of using tools and symbols to gather information from the Collective Unconsciousness. This can be on people, places, things and events past, present, and future.

Divine Power: The un-manifested, pure energy that exists within the Goddess and God. The life force, the ultimate source of all things.

Dogon: Tribe in Mali, Africa, who inexplicably seem to have knowledge of the invisible companion of the star Sirius, which cannot be seen without a telescope.

Doppelgänger: "Double walker" in German, an existence of a spirit doubles, or ghosts an exact but usually invisible replica of a living person or any other sort of physical double. Seeing one's own doppelgänger is an omen of death.

Doty, Sergeant Richard C. Air Force Office of Special Investigations - Served in Laos & Vietnam. Later transferred to AFOSI & was assigned to Kirtland AFB. Investigated Weitzel UFO sighting & Paul Bennewitz. Later served in West Germany. After retiring from USAF, became a New Mexico Highway Patrolman. A friend and/or associate of William L. Moore.

Dowsing: The divinatory art of using a pendulum or stick to find the actual location of a person, place, thing, or element. See Ideomotor Effect.

Drawing Down the Moon: A ritual performed during the Full Moon by witches to empower themselves and unite their essence with a particular deity, usually the Goddess.

Drawing Down the Sun: Lesser-known and lesser-used companion ritual to Drawing Down the Moon in which the essence of the Sun God is drawn into the body of a male witch.

Dreamland: Another name for Area 51. It's the term used by the Nellis AFB control tower to refer to the base.

Duality: The opposite of polarity. When used as a religious term, it separates two opposites such as good and evil and places those characteristics into two completely separate God-forms.

Dulce: While investigating cattle mutilations on the Jicarillo Indian Reservation outside Dulce, New Mexico, Paul Bennewitz saw mysterious objects rising from Mt. Archuleta. He wrongfully assumed, or was misled into believing, that there was an alien base inside the mountain. Others have added to the story since, and the Dulce base has become legendary.

E

Earthquake Lights: Lights, which sometimes appear just before or during an earthquake.

Earth Magick: The energy that exists within stones, herbs, flames, wind, and other natural objects.

Earth Plane: Metaphor for your normal waking consciousness, or for the everyday, solid world we live in.

Ectoplasm: Is a solid or vaporous substance, lifelike and moldable, that supposedly exudes from the body of a medium (usually from one of the facial orifices) to form seemingly corporeal limbs, faces, or entire bodies. Ectoplasm is a usually dense but liquidity, milky-white substance with the scent of ozone. It can also be the residue left behind by ghosts or other paranormal phenomena. Many experts believe that spirits use ectoplasm to materialize.

Electromagnetic Field (EMF): A measurable field of electrical energy. Some believe that anomalous shifts in the electromagnetic field can be evidence of a ghost attempting to manifest. Others believe that ghosts are drawn to low-level electromagnetic fields.
See Ghost.

Electromagnetic Field Meter (EMF Meter): Electricians' use these meters to check for bad wiring, and are typically calibrated to detect frequencies within the range of alternating current from the factory. Therefor testing and recalibrating these devices are not possible or a requirement for an electricians' tool dealing with typical 110 - 240 volts from an US household outlet. Scientific devices to ensure the accuracy of the data must be tested, and recalibrated each time it is used. After once we understand how these devises work, knowing that flashy lights look good on television. In all reality serves no purpose outside of its intended use.

Electronic Voice Phenomenon (EVP): A method of Instrumental communication wherein human ears do not immediately hear anomalous disembodied voices. Capture by sound recording equipment that when listened to later with the use of specialized audio software.

Elements: Usually: Earth, air, fire, water. The building blocks of the universe. Everything that exists contains one or more of these energies. Some include a fifth element- spirit or Akasha.

Elementals: Archetypical spirit beings associated with one of the four elements. Also, see Faeries.

Eleven: Secretive tradition of the craft, which works closely with elemental beings.

ELF: Extremely Low Frequency range between 3-3,000Hz borders on DC as well as AC.

Elysium/Elysian Fields: (Greek mythology) the abode of the blessed after death.

Enchantment: A magickal object that must be kept absolutely secret, and hidden from all human eyes. This affects a hidden aura. They must be charmed first. Gems and magickal writing are good items to use.

Entity: Intelligent, parasitic, energy-based life forms that can possess or inhabit a physical life form to control it and feed off its life force until the host die. Also, see Ghost.

Eostre's Eggs: Colored, decorated eggs of Ostara; named for the Teutonic Goddess Eostre.

Epistemological: A branch of philosophy concerned with the nature and scope of knowledge, and referred to as "theory of knowledge".

Esbat: A ritual usually occurring on the Full Moon and dedicated to the Goddess in her lunar aspect.

Estimate of the Situation: In 1948, Project Sign personnel thought it time to make a formal Estimate of the Situation giving the results of their investigation of UFOs so far. This was sent to Air Force Chief of Staff General Hoyt Vandenberg, who rejected the report's conclusion that UFOs were extraterrestrial in origin. He ordered the report destroyed.

Etherealology: The study of unworldly, spiritual or ghostly, heavenly or celestial.

Evocation: To call something out from within.

Exeter: City in New Hampshire that was the site of a wave of UFO sightings beginning in September 1965. Book: Incident at Exeter by John G. Fuller.

Exorcism: The expulsion of a ghost, spirit, demon, or other entity/entities thought to possess or haunt a human being or location. The ritual, conducted by an exorcist, is usually religious in nature, and calls upon some Higher Power to cast out the evil force(s).

Extraterrestrial Biological Entity (EBE) The seventeenth episode of the first season of the American science fiction television series; The X-Files. See Roswell Incident, and Aliens Grays.

Extrasensory Perception (ESP): The paranormal sensing of sight, sound, taste, smell and touch. ESP is divided into three categories, telepathy, clairvoyance and precognition. ESP occurs in mediumship, possession, cases of apparitions, some cases of poltergeists, hauntings, near-death experiences and out-of-body experiences.

F

Fear Cage: (Paranormal) A confined or localized area with unhealthily high levels of electromagnetic radiation due to the presence of a large amount of electrical devices, unshielded electrical cables, or power junctions. Individuals with sensitivity to Electromagnetic Fields (EMF) can experience sensations of anxiety, paranoia, or nausea after prolonged exposure to these places. They report feelings of "being watched" and this effect often gives rise to sincere but unsubstantiated claims of haunting.

Face on Mars: A mysterious plateau in the Cydonia area of Mars that looks like a face in some photos. Some say it must have been created by intelligent life. NASA says it's a natural formation combined with a trick of light.

Faerie: See Elemental

Faerie Burgh: Mound of earth, which covers a faerie colony's underground home.

Falcon Lake: lake in Whiteshell Provincial Park, Manitoba, Canada, where, in 1967 prospector Stephen Michalak had a close encounter with a UFO that left him with burns across his chest.

Falsifiable: (Science) confirmable: capable of being tested (verified or falsified) by experiment or observation.

Familiar (familiar spirit): A spirit that takes animal form that protects, and serves. Having a spiritual bond with a witch also refers to flesh-and-blood figures, including a companion. Familiars can also be entities that dwell on the astral plane.

Fascination: A mental effort to control another animal or person's mind. Also known as "mind-bending". Often considered unethical.

Fata Morgana: A type of mirage that seems to be a castle or a city floating on the ocean.

Fetch: In Irish and English folklore, the term for one's double, an apparition of a living person.
Also, see Doppelgänger.

Fermi Paradox: A question first asked by physicist Enrico Fermi - "If there are intelligent extraterrestrials out there, why haven't they contacted us?"

Feuerball: Supposedly a flying craft developed by the Nazis during World War II.

Firmage, Joe: Former CEO of USWeb, who quit to form the International Space Sciences Organization and to write The Truth, about UFOs and space travel, among other things.

Flatwoods, West Virginia: Site of a burning object crash and sightings of a mysterious creature in 1952.

Flight 19: Ill-fated group of five avenger aircraft on a training mission from Fort Lauderdale, Florida. Disappeared in the Bermuda Triangle in 1945.

Flying Saucer: (UFOlogy) this is a name for certain types of UFOs. It originated when Kenneth Arnold described the objects that he saw as looking like a "saucer skipping across water."

Folklore: Traditional sayings, cures, faerie tales, and folk wisdom of a particular locale, which is separate from their mythology.

Folk Magick: The Practice of projecting personal power, as well as the energies within natural objects such as herbs, and crystals, to bring about needed changes.

Foo Fighters: (UFOlogy) During World War II, both sides reported strange lights and objects flying alongside their planes. Each side at first believed they were some kind of a new secret weapon belonging to the other side. No explanation was ever found. The name foo fighter comes from a WWII cartoon character named "Smoky Stover" who said where there is foo there is fire!

Ford, John: President of the Long Island UFO Network. Arrested in 1996 for conspiring to poison local officials with radium.

Forensic science: The application of a broad spectrum of sciences and technologies to investigate situations after the fact and to establish what occurred based on collected evidence.

Fort, Charles: (1874 - 1932) the first UFOlogist & investigator of unusual phenomena. Author of several books including The Book of the Damned and Lo!

Foundation for Research on the Nature of Man (FRNM): See Rhine Research Center.

Fowler, Raymond: Alien Abduction researcher and author Allagash Abductions, among others. Better known for his book, The Andreasson Affair: The Documented Investigation of a Woman's Abduction aboard a UFO. Betty Andreasson Luca first abduction occurred during her childhood and culminated with an abduction experience that involved her whole family. Led by a number of teams of highly credentialed investigators, her experience is one of the most thoroughly investigated cases ever reported in the annals of hypnotherapy.

Fox Sisters: (Paranormal) Leah (1814–1890), Margaret (also called Maggie) (1833–1893) and Kate Fox (1837–1892) In March 31, 1848 events, which took place with the Fox family, home in Hydesville, New York, and considered to have initiated the Modern Spiritualist Movement. They all enjoyed success as mediums for many years. The two younger sisters used "rapping" to convince their much older sister and others that they were communicating with spirits. Their older sister then took charge of them and managed their careers for some time. In 1888, Margaret confessed that their rapping had been a hoax and publicly demonstrated their method. She attempted to recant her confession the next year, but their reputation was ruined and in less than five years, they were all dead, with Margaret and Kate dying in abject poverty.

Freemasonry is a fraternal organization that traces its origins to the local fraternities of stonemasons, which from the end of the fourteenth century regulated the qualifications of masons and their interaction with authorities and clients. The degrees of freemasonry, its gradual system, retain the three grades of medieval craft guilds, those of Apprentice, journeyman or fellow (now called Fellow Craft), and Master Mason. These are the degrees offered by craft, or blue lodge Freemasonry. See Masonic Lodge, Shriners.

Friedrich Juergenson: Swedish film producer, while recording bird song in a forest for an upcoming movie, first discovered the now called Electronic Voice

Phenomenon EVP. He heard two very faint but audible voices while playing back the recording he had made through a reel-to-reel machine. The first was the voice of a man speaking of the bird song at night, and the other was that of his mother calling him by his nickname and saying he was being watched over.

Friedman, Stanton: Physicist formerly worked for Westinghouse. Author of Crash at Corona (With Don Berliner), and Top Secret/Majic. One of the primary investigators of the Roswell Incident and the MJ-12 documents

G

Gaea/Gaia: (Belief) Mother Earth.

Gaussmeter: (Tesla meters) Measure the magnetic field at a point in space. They can be divided into scalar devices, which only measure the intensity of the field, and vector devices, which also measure the direction of the field. See Magnetometer.

> **Hall Effect** devices convert the energy stored in a magnetic field to an electrical signal by developing a voltage between the two edges of a current-carrying conductor whose faces are perpendicular to a magnetic field.
>
> **Magnetodiodes** are two-terminal Hall Effect devices similar to a conventional bipolar diode. The voltage-current characteristic of a magnetodiode is sensitive to a magnetic field.
>
> **Magnetotransistors** consist of a bipolar transistor implemented on a semiconductor surface. They are three-pronged devices consisting of an emitter region, an elongated base region, and a collector region. The presence of a magnetic field in the base region creates a Hall Effect voltage, which produces a pulse on the transmission line.

Geryon: (Mythology) a mythical monster with three heads that was slain by Hercules.

Ghost Rockets: Many unidentified aerial objects were reported over Scandinavia in 1946 - 1947. They looked like missiles with a flame exhaust at one end flying at various speeds. They were thought to be Russian missile tests, but this was never verified.

Ghost Lights: See Spook-lights, Ignis Fatuus.

Ghost: Disembodied pattern of consciousness that interacts with the material world in a seemingly intelligent or organized manner.

Ghost Hunters: The SyFy series that started on October 6, 2004, following TAPS paranormal investigations through allegedly haunted locations. See TAPS.

Ghost in Bachelors Grove Cemetery, Chicago: On August 10, 1991, several members of the Ghost Research Society (GRS) edge of the Rubio Woods Forest Cemetery Preserve, a suburb of Midlothian, Illinois. The cemetery had been considered the most haunted in the U.S., therefore GRS team came to investigate about it.

Ghosts Railroad Crossing in San Antonio, Texas: The site of a horrible accident, where several schoolchildren were killed when the bus stalled on the railroad tracks. Since that dreadful accident many years ago, any car stopped near the railroad tracks will be pushed by unseen hands across the tracks to safety. The legend is that if a light powder - like talcum or baby powder is sprinkled over the car's trunk and rear bumper, tiny fingerprints and handprints will appear, the prints of the ghost children pushing the car out of harm's way.

Ghostbusters: A 1984 film stars Bill Murray, Dan Aykroyd and Harold Ramis as three eccentric parapsychologists in New York City, who start a ghost catching business. (Term) Paranormal for teams that rids the location from Ghosts.

Ghost Groupies: Are paranormal enthusiast that are only interested is going ghost hunting. These groups show a lack of professionalism and commitment to serious research.

Gill, Father William Booth: Anglican missionary who reported UFOs over Boianai, Papua, New Guinea in 1959.

Glossolalia: Speaking in tongues is the fluid vocalizing (or less commonly the writing) of speech-like syllables that lack any readily comprehended meaning, in some cases as part of religious practice

Goblin: A small, ugly, evil spirit.

God: Masculine aspect of deity.

Goddess: Feminine aspect of deity.

Gorgon: (Mythology) any of three winged sister monsters and the mortal Medusa who had live snakes for hair; a glance at Medusa turned the beholder to stone.

Grace: (Greek mythology) one of three sisters who were the givers of beauty and charm; a favorite subject for sculptors.

Grain Dolly: Figure usually woven at Imbolc from dried sheaves of grain collected at the previous harvest. The dolly traditionally burned at Yule and a new one made the following Imbolc.

Gray Lady: Is the ghost of a woman whose death that caused by a loved one, or who died while waiting for her lover to return.

Great Rite: Symbolic sexual union (also sacred marriage) of the Goddess and God that enacted at Beltane in many traditions, and other Sabbats in other traditions. It symbolizes the primal act of creation from which all life comes.

Green Man: A symbol of rebirth, representing the cycle of growth each spring.

Gremlin: A small, annoying spirit, generally friendly in nature, given to mischief and pranks involving electrical and mechanical equipment. Gremlins appear to be particularly fond of aircraft, and the British Royal Air Force in World War I first acknowledged them after pilots on dangerous missions reported seeing misty, goblin-like spirits in their aircraft.

Grimorie: A magickal workbook containing ritual information, formulae, magickal properties of natural objects and preparation of ritual equipment. Often used interchangeably with Book of Shadows.

Grounding: To disperse excess energy generated during magickal work by sending it into the earth. It also means the process of centering one's self in the physical world both before and after any ritual or astral experience.

Grove: Synonymous with coven.

Green Fireballs: Objects seen in the skies of New Mexico, mainly in 1948 -1949. They had the appearance of brilliant green balls of light. Project Twinkle was set up to study them. They were never explained, but the best theory seems to be that they were some type of meteorite.

Groom Lake: See Area 51.

Grudge, Project: In 1949, Project Grudge, the second Air Force UFO investigation, replaced Project Sign. Its name reflected its attitude. It mainly sought to debunk UFO sightings.

Gruenwald, Scott: Known better as "The STU" and for STUCon paranormal convention. Paranormal Investigator, Actor & Reporter on the TV Series Paranormal Paparazzi, and has appeared on Paranormal Challenge, Ghost Adventures, and Ghost Hunters paranormal reality television series, and the investigation of Wolfe Manor in Clovis California.

Guardians: Ceremonial magicians use the Guardians of the Watchtowers or Four Quarters. Some witches use them, too.

H

Hallucination: A false or distorted perception of objects or events with a full belief in their reality.

Hand Fasting: A Pagan wedding.

Harris, Paola L. Is an Italian-American photojournalist and investigative reporter in the field of extraterrestrial related phenomena research. She has studied extraterrestrial related phenomena since 1979 and is on personal terms with many of the leading researchers in the field. She returned to Roswell in the summer of 2003 for the American debut of her book; **Connecting the Dots; Making Sense of the UFO Phenomenon.**

Haunting: A state of being wherein research and evaluation cannot explain away multiple consistent anomalous occurrences. Sometimes mistaken conclusions drawn that certain events taking place at or about the location are of paranormal origin.

Haunted house: A house that believed to be the center of supernatural or paranormal occurrences.

Hawes, Jason: founder see TAPS.

Healing (psychic): Healing apparently brought about through a paranormal, non-medical means, such as prayer, the "laying on of hands," immersion at a religious shrine, and so on. It is inexplicable to contemporary medical science.

Hebe: (Mythology) is the goddess of youth, the cupbearer for the gods and goddesses of Mount Olympus, serving their nectar and ambrosia, until she was married to Heracles. The daughter of Zeus and Hera.

Helen of Troy: (Mythology) was the daughter of Zeus and Leda, and was a sister of Castor, Pollux, and Clytemnestra. In Greek myths, considered the most beautiful woman in the world. Her abduction by Paris brought about the Trojan War.

Hephaestus: (Mythology) is the Greek god of blacksmiths, craftsmen, artisans, sculptors, metals, metallurgy, fire and volcanoes. The son of Zeus and Hera.

Hercules: (Roman Mythology) known as **Heracles:** (Greek Mythology) also known as Hercules, with whom the later Roman Emperors, in particular Commodus and Maximian, often identified themselves.

Herbalism: Art of using herbs to facilitate human needs both magickally and medicinally.

Hermes: (Mythology) protector and patron of travelers, herdsmen, thieves, orators and wit, literature and poets, athletics and sports, invention and trade. In some myths, he is a trickster, and outwits other gods for his own satisfaction or the sake of humankind.

Hertz unit of frequency defined as the number of cycles per second, and named for Heinrich Rudolf Hertz.

Hz is the unit of measurement for frequencies.

Higher Self: That part of us, which connects our corporeal minds to the Collective Unconscious and with the divine knowledge of the universe.

Hill, Betty and Barney: Married couple who were purportedly abducted from their car by aliens in the White Mountains of New Hampshire in 1961. He was a postal worker and she was a social worker. Called the first "modern" abductees.

Hiving Off: This term used for a small coven, which splits off from a larger one. Sometimes this is done to keep the gatherings of a manageable size, other times covens split over philosophical differences.

Holzer, Dr. Hans (26 January 1920 – 26 April 2009) earned his PhD from the London College of Applied Science. An Austrian-born, American pioneering in paranormal researcher and author well over 100 books, and is most famous for investigating the Amityville Horror house. Called the father of Ghost Hunting investigating some of the most prominent haunted locations around the world.

Homer: The author of the Iliad and the Odyssey, and is revered as the greatest of ancient Greek epic poets. These epics lie at the beginning of the Western canon of literature, and have had an enormous influence on the history of literature.

Hopkins, Budd: Abduction researcher and author. His books include Missing Time, Intruders, and Witnessed!

Horned God: One of the most prevalent God-images in Paganism. NOT Satan or the Devil, which are Christion concepts.

Hudson Valley: Area of New York State that was the site of a series of UFO sightings beginning in 1983.

HYNEK UFO SIGHTINGS CLASSIFICATION SYSTEM

Hynek, J. Allen: Astronomer, Professor of Astronomy at Ohio State University (1935 - 1953); Advisor to Project Grudge(1948) - 1952; Advisor to Project Bluebook (1952 - 1969); Associate Director of the Smithsonian Astrophysical Laboratory at Harvard (1956 - 1960);Professor of Astronomy at Northwestern

University (1960 - 1978) In 1973, he founded CUFOS, the Center for UFO studies.

Hypnagogic: The transitional state of consciousness experienced while falling asleep sometimes characterized by vivid hallucinations or imagery; also sometimes used to refer to the similar state of awareness experienced during the process of awakening.

Hypnopompic: The transitional state of consciousness experienced while awakening; sometimes called hypnagogic state.

Hypnosis: An artificially induced altered state of consciousness, characterized by heightened suggestibility and receptivity to direction.

I

Ignis Fatuus: Literally meaning "foolish fire," ignis fatuus are any of a variety of ghost or spectral lights. According to some folkloric traditions, the lights are souls of the dead; in other legends, they are imp-like spirits.

Ideomotor Effect: Refers to the influence of suggestion or expectation on involuntary and unconscious motor behavior. The movement of pointers on Ouija boards, of a facilitator's hands in facilitated communication, of hands and arms in applied kinesiology, and of some behaviors attributed to hypnotic suggestion, are due to ideomotor action.

Illinois, Lebanon and Millstadt: Several police officers in this area saw a large UFO on the night of January 5, 2000.

Illuminati: (illuminatus, "enlightened") is a name given to several groups, both real and fictitious. Historically the name refers to the Bavarian Illuminati, an Enlightenment-era secret society founded on May 1, 1776 to oppose superstition, prejudice, religious influence over public life, abuses of state power, and to support women's education and gender equality, and refers to various organizations claiming or purported to have unsubstantiated links to the original Bavarian Illuminati or similar secret societies, and often alleged to conspire to control world affairs by masterminding events and planting agents in government and corporations to establish a New World Order.

Illusion: Constructed to be wrongly perceive or misinterpreted by the senses. While Magicians use misdirection. The Illusionists involve unlikely bystanders; everyone is in on the trick, except you.

Imprinting: A ghost can attach its energy to an item of a personal nature, imprinting itself on the object. The energy imprint can remain, though objects are moved long distances.

Incense: Ritual burning of herbs, oils, or other aromatic items to scent the air during acts of magick and ritual, and to better help the witch attune to the goal of the working.

Incubus: A male demon believed to lie on sleeping persons and to have sexual intercourse with sleeping women.

Institute of Spectrological Research - ISR is an Anomalies Research and Educational Organization established in 2011 to study anomalous spectrological phenomena based on experimentation, observations, and field research. Educating the public on the unexplained by providing alternative explanations to what people are mistakenly assuming as spectro-paranormal.

ULTIMATE PARANORMAL GUIDE

Intelligent Entity: A supernatural being that evidences intelligence and will of its own.

Intelligent Haunting: This type of haunt is when the entity is aware of the living world and interacts with or responds to it. The entity is able to communicate with the living, not just by talking, but also by moving inanimate objects such as furniture or other objects.

International Society of Cryptozoology ISC, which is dedicated to searching for animal species not recognized by conventional science. Members of the group have organized expeditions into the wilderness of Northern California in search of Bigfoot, and to Scotland in pursuit of the Loch Ness Monster.

Initiation: A process whereby an individual is introduced or admitted into a coven. Usually a ritual occasion. Not to be confused with dedication.

Invocation: To bring something in from without.

Irwin, Private Gerry: Nike missile technician from Fort Bliss, who had an odd experience after seeing an object land in a field in 1959. He later deserted and vanished.

J

Jacobs, David M.: Abduction researcher and author. His books include The Threat and Secret Life.

JAL1628: Japan Airlines 747 that was followed by a UFO over Alaska in 1986.

James, Peter: (Sep. 24 192?-30 died July 31 2007) Psychic, and Paranormal Investigator famous for communicating with spirits including the talking ghost child 'Jackie' on Queen Mary. Unexplained Mysteries, Sightings, and hosted paranormal evening tours aboard the Queen Mary in 1992. See Gian Temperilli.

James Randi Educational Foundation works to inspire this investigative spirit in a new generation of critical thinkers. Founded in 1996 to help people defend themselves from paranormal and pseudo-scientific claims. The JREF offers a still-unclaimed million-dollar reward for anyone who can produce evidence of paranormal abilities under controlled conditions.

Japan Extraterrestrial Intelligence Center -JCETI established in 2010 to spread the correct understanding extraterrestrial intelligent (ETI). The organization is active in education. Its main activities are lectures and workshops CE-5 contact (fifth kind close encounter activities), confidential information UFO disclosure.

Jessup, Morris K.: Astronomer and author of UFO books, notably The Case for The UFO. Committed suicide in 1959. Also, see The Philadelphia Experiment

Jew-itch: Name coined by some Pagans of Jewish origin who are actively seeking out the pagan roots of their birth religion.

Jinn/Jinnī/Genie: A spiritual creature both good and evil in Islam and Arabic folklore. See Ghost.

Jupiter: Chief god in Roman mythology.

Jürgenson, Friedrich: Swedish painter and film producer was recording bird songs. When he listen to recording, he had to tape his dead mother's voice that had addressed him by his nickname: "Friedel, can you hear me? Here's mommy." Jürgenson made over 100,000 recordings, which he described as being communications with discarnate people. He published his book, "Voices from Space" in 1964. Also, see Electronic Voice Phenomenon (EVP).

K

Kabbalah: Mystical teaching from the Jewish-Gnostic tradition. Ceremonial Magick and the Alexandrian traditions are based in these teachings. Also, Qabala.

Karma: The belief that one's thoughts and deeds can be either counted against them or added to their spiritual path across several life times.

Kecksburg, Pennsylvania: Site of a mysterious crash of an object in 1966.

Kelly - Hopkinsville, Kentucky: Site where the Sutton family was beseiged by "goblins" in 1955.

Keyhoe, Major Donald E.: U.S. Marine Corps. An aide to Charles Lindbergh. Began writing about UFOs for True magazine in 1949. Author: The Flying Saucers are real, published in 1950. Later director of NICAP from 1957 to 1969.

K-II: (Paranormal) EM device designed to pick up AC manmade power sources in walls by lighting up a series of lights from green to red. Adopted for uses in the paranormal field to communicate with the dead. In reality serves no purpose outside its intended use.

Kirlian photography: A type of high-voltage, high-frequency photography developed in the Soviet Union by Davidovich Kirlian, which captures an individual's aura.

Kugelblitz: Supposedly a flying craft developed by the Nazis during World War II.

L

Labrys: A double-headed ax, which symbolizes the Goddess in Her Lunar aspect. Has roots in ancient Crete.

Lago de Cote: A lake in Costa Rica over which a government-mapping camera on board an aircraft took an unexplained photo of an apparent UFO in 1971.

Lagrange Points: Points in the orbit of a body around another body where their gravities are in equilibrium.

Laveau, Marie (September 10, 1794 – June 16, 1881) was a Louisiana Creole practitioner of Voodoo renowned in New Orleans. Reported to have had 15 children her daughter Marie Laveau II, who sometimes used the surname "Paris" after her mother's first husband. Immortalized in story and song, she was said to have possessed immense power, which lives on through her spirit today.

> **Laveau II, Marie** (1827 - 1895) daughter of Marie Laveau also practiced Voudoun Haitian Voodoo.

Lazar, Robert "Bob": UFO personality. Claimed to be a physicist who was hired by Edward Teller to reverse-engineer a UFO at Papoose Lake, near Area 51.

Lear, John: Ex-CIA pilot. Son of Edward Lear, of Lear Jet fame. UFO personality & conspiracy theorist.

Left-Hand Path: Refers to the practice of using magick to control others, to change the will of others, for personal gain. Generally frowned upon by true Wiccans and Witch's. Dark Magick.

Levitation: The raising or suspension of persons or objects in the air in such a means as violates the known physical laws of motion and gravity.

Libation: Ritually given portion of food or drink to a deity, nature spirit, or ghost.

LIUFON: The Long Island UFO Network.

Loch Ness Monster: (Cryptozoology) On April 14, 1933, a couple spotted an unknown animal as they drove past Loch Ness in the Scottish Highlands. There were suggestions in 1933 that the creature resembled the supposedly extinct plesiosaur. In 2004, a documentary team for television channel five, using special effects experts from movies, tried to make people believe there was something in the loch. They constructed an animatronic model of a plesiosaur, and dubbed it "Lucy". Despite setbacks, such as Lucy falling to the bottom of the loch, about 600 sightings were reported in the places they conducted the hoaxes. Scientists largely believe the Loch Ness Monster is a myth or a hoax.

Loedding, Alfred: member of Project Sign. Designer of unusual aircraft.

Long-Distance Echoes: A radio phenomenon in which transmissions are reflected back to Earth by some unknown mechanism.

Loring AFB, Maine: U.S. Air Force Base. Site of some unusual UFO events on 27 October 1975.

Lucid dream: A dream in which the dreamer is conscious of the fact they are dreaming.

M

Mack, John: Harvard psychiatrist and abduction researcher. Author of Abduction - Human Encounters with Aliens.

Mackal, Roy P. Cryptozoologist (born August 1, 1925), reportedly died September 13, 2013 at the age of 88. Retired University of Chicago biologist best known to the public for his interest in the Loch Ness Monster and other cryptozoological entities.

Macrocosm: The world around us.

Magick: The projection of natural energies (such as personal power) to being about needed change. Energy exists in all things: us, plants, stones, colors, sounds, movements, words. Magick is the process of raising this energy, giving it purpose, and releasing it. Magick is a natural, not supernatural, practice, but is little understood. Magick is neither black nor white. It simply is. What the magician decides to do with the magick is another matter...

Magick Circle: A sphere constructed of personal power in which rituals are usually performed. Within it, the witch is protected from outside forces. The sphere extends both above and below the surface of the ground.

Magickal System: The basic set of guidelines relating to the worship of specific Gods and Goddesses or cultural traditions.

Magnetometers: Measurement instruments used for two general purposes to measure the magnetization of a magnetic material like a ferromagnet, or to measure the strength and, in some cases, the direction of the magnetic field at a point in space. Also known as a gaussmeter or survey magnetometer.
See Gaussmeters.

Scalar

These magnetometers measure magnitude only.

> **Proton** precession devices use liquids such as kerosene and methanol that have high densities of hydrogen atoms.

> **Optically pumped** instruments polarize a gaseous alkali with a specific wavelength of light. An RF signal is modulated to determine its optimum depolarization frequency - this depolarization frequency varies with the ambient magnetic field.

> **Overhauser** or nuclear precession devices combine an electron-rich liquid with hydrogen and then subject the mixture to a radio frequency (RF) signal.

Vector

There magnetometers measure both magnitude and direction.

SQUIDs or superconducting quantum interference devices consists of two superconductors separated by thin insulating layers to form two parallel Josephson junctions. They are most commonly used to measure the magnetic fields produced by brain or heart activity.

Atomic SERF magnetometers achieve very high magnetic field sensitivity by monitoring a high-density vapor of alkali metal atoms processing in a near-zero magnetic field. They are among the most sensitive magnetic field sensors available.

Flux gate or coil instruments measure differences in the magnetic field at the ends of a vertical rod and plot this information on a grid.

Magnetoinductive devices consist of a coil that surrounds a ferromagnetic core whose permeability changes within the earth's magnetic field.

Majestic-12: Supposedly a group of twelve high-ranking scientists, military leaders, and government officials that was formed by executive order of President Harry Truman to investigate the UFO phenomenon. MJ-12 was first brought to public attention with the 1987 release of the MJ-12 documents. These documents purported to be copies of top-secret documents given by an anonymous "insider" to film producer Jaime Shandera.

Male Mysteries: Pagan study which attempts to reclaim the power and mystery of the old Gods for today's Pagan males.

Malmstrom AFB, Montana: U.S. Air Force base in Montana. Site of unusual UFO events in 1966, 1967, and 1975.

Mansfield, Ohio: Town where Lawrence J. Coyne & others aboard a National Guard helicopter had a close brush with a UFO in 1973.

Mantell, Captain Thomas: Pilot who crashed near Fort Knox, Kentucky while chasing a UFO.

Marcel, Major Jesse: Intelligence officer at Roswell Army Air Base who investigated the Roswell crash in July 1947.

Marfa: A town west Texas that is a famed spook-light site. The lights seen in the nearby mountains and are known as the Marfa Lights.

Marian: The appearance of the ghostlike figure of the Virgin Mary, mother of Jesus.

Matrixing: See Pareidolia.

Matrifocal: Term used to denote pre-patriarchal life when family clans centered around and lived near or on clan matriarch.

Maury Island: Island in Puget Sound near Tacoma, Washington where two men claimed to have seen UFOs in June 1947. Regarded as a hoax.

May Pole: Sexual symbol of Beltane representing the phallus.

McDonald, James E. Professor of meteorology at the University of Arizona. Staunch supporter of a formal scientific investigation of UFOs. Called for congressional investigation of UFOs. Author: Science in Default: Twenty-two Years of Inadequate UFO Investigations. Committed suicide in 1971.

Mesmerism: The original term for hypnotism, named after Austrian physician Franz Anton Mesmer (1733-1815).

Metaphysics: A field of study dedicated to the nature of reality.

Mel-8704: (Paranormal) Device that measure EMF and temperature. Gary Galka (designer) named the device after his daughter Melissa who died in an automobile accident. See EMF & Calibration.

Men In Black (MIB) are a supposed group of individuals who dress in black suits and drive black cars. They are said to threaten people who have UFO encounters in order to deter them from talking about the incident.

Mexico City, 1991: During the solar eclipse on July 11, 1991, camcorder enthusiasts in Mexico captured inexplicable images of a UFO on videotape.

Meditation: Reflection, contemplation- turning inward toward the self, or outward toward Deity or nature. A quiet time in which the practitioner may either dwell upon particular thoughts or symbols, or allow them to come unbidden.

Medium: Someone who can communicate with spirits on behalf of another living being. The word suggests that the medium acts as a midway point, halfway between the worlds of the living and the dead.

Megalith: A huge stone monument or structure. Stonehenge is the best-known example of a megalith.

ULTIMATE PARANORMAL GUIDE

Menhir: A huge stone probably erected by early peoples for religious, spiritual, or magickal reasons.

Microcosm: The world within us.

Michilak, Stephen: Prospector who had a close encounter with a UFO in 1967 at Falcon Lake in Whiteshell Provincial Park, Manitoba, Canada, that left him with burns across his chest.

Milligauss – Unit of measurement of magnetic fields. 1 gauss = 1 Mx/cm2 this unit is named after Carl Friedrich Gauss. See Gaussmeter & Magnetometer.

> **mG** = Milligauss – a unit of measurement of a magnetic field equal to one thousandth of 1 gauss.

> **mV** = millivolt - a unit of potential equal to one thousandth of a volt.

Minos: (Mythology) was a king of Crete, son of Zeus and Europa. Every nine years, he made King Aegeus pick seven young boys and seven young girls to be sent to Daedalus' creation, the labyrinth, to be eaten by the Minotaur. After his death, Minos became a judge of the dead in the underworld.

Missing Time: Those who see UFOs sometimes discover that there are periods of time that they cannot account for. Regression hypnosis sometimes reveals that aliens abducted them during these periods of missing time.

MJ-12 documents. Had a group of contacts within the government and the military whom he gave bird code names and whom he referred to as the Aviary.

MKUltra: is the code name of a U.S. government human research operation experimenting in the behavioral engineering of humans through the CIA's Scientific Intelligence Division. The program engaged in many illegal activities; in particular, it used unwitting U.S. and Canadian citizens as its test subjects, which led to controversy regarding its legitimacy, and officially halted in 1973.

Mnemosyne: (Mythology) the daughter of Gaia and Uranus and the mother of the 9 Muses by Zeus:

> **Calliope** (Epic Poetry)
> **Clio** (History)
> **Erato** (Love Poetry)
> **Euterpe** (Music)
> **Melpomene** (Tragedy)
> **Polyhymnia** (Hymns)
> **Terpsichore** (Dance)
> **Thalia** (Comedy)
> **Urania** (Astronomy)

Monotheism: Belief in one supreme deity who has no other forms and/or displays no other aspects.

Mogul, Project: A top-secret 1947 project that used high-altitude balloons to attempt to detect Soviet nuclear tests.

Moriches Bay, Long Island: Site where the U.S. allegedly shot down and recovered a UFO in 1989. Also site of the TWA Flight 800 disaster in 1996.

Moses, William Stainton (1839-1892) occupies a special position in spiritualism and psychic research. While a convinced spiritualist was skeptical of psychic photography. In 1875 identified defects in the Brown Lady picture. Having seen as many as 600 alleged spirit photographs he declared: "Some people would recognize anything. A broom and a sheet are quite enough for some wild enthusiasts who go with the figure in their eye and see what they wish to see... I have had pictures that might be anything in this or any other world gravely claimed as recognized portraits." Initially, like most of the clergy, he was deeply hostile to the notion of spirits of the dead being conjured up by trance mediums

Mother: The aspect of the Goddess representing motherhood, mid-life, and fertility. The full moon, the egg, and the colors red and green represent her. Her Sabbats are Midsummer and Lughnasadh.

Mother goddess: Used to refer to a goddess who represents motherhood, fertility, creation, or who embodies the bounty of the Earth

Mothership: Some observers have reported large UFOs out of which smaller craft seem to come. Sort of like a UFO "aircraft carrier."

Mokele-mbembe: an alleged living dinosaur in the Likouala swamp region of the Republic of Congo. Congo natives, who, consistently reported describing a creature similar to a long-necked sauropod.

Moncla, Lieutenant Felix: Air Force F-89 pilot who, along with his navigator Lieutenant R. R. Wilson, disappeared while chasing a UFO over Lake Superior in 1953.

Montauk Project: Purported government time-travel experiment that took place at Montauk Air Station on Long Island. Related to The Philadelphia Experiment.

Moore, William L. Writer, former schoolteacher. Member of NICAP and APRO. A co-author, with Charles Berlitz, of the Philadelphia Experiment: Project Invisibility and the Roswell Incident. Which also involved Paul Bennewtiz with his friend and/or associate of Richard S. Doty, Stanton Friedman, and Jaime Shandera.

Mothman: A mysterious winged creature who appeared around Point Pleasant, West Virginia in 1966 - 1967.

MUFON: The Mutual UFO Network. The largest UFO organization in the world.

Muse: (Mythology) the goddesses of the inspiration of literature, science, poetry, and the arts. They were considered the source of the knowledge, related orally for centuries in the ancient culture that was contained in poetic lyrics and myths. See Mnemosyne.

Myth: Cycles Body of stories about any land or people that makes up their culture.

Mythology: The study of traditional beliefs, folklore, and legends from the ancient Greek, and Roman cultures. The epic tales of Gods, Goddesses, Monsters, and Heroes.

Mythology Classical: The system of mythology of the Greeks and Romans together; much of Roman mythology (especially the gods) was borrowed from the Greeks.

Mythomania: An abnormal or pathological tendency to exaggerate or tell lies. See Pseudologia fantastica.

N

National Institute for Discovery Science: Founded in 1995 by Robert Bigelow set up the organization to advance serious study of various fringe science, and paranormal topics, most notably ufology. The NIDSci disbanded in October 2004.

nm = Nanometer one-billionth of a meter (1 x 10-9 m).

Near Death Experience (NDE): An experience that has reported by people who clinically die, or come close to actual death and are revived. These events often include encounters with spirit guides, seeing dead relatives or friends, life review, out-of-body-experiences (OBE), or a moment of decision where they are able to decide or told to turn back.

Necromancy/Necromancer: A form of prophecy, in which the seer or sorcerer/sorceress raises the spirit (though not usually the corporal remains) of the dead in order to have the wraith foretell future events. It was thought that upon entering eternity, the spirit would have full knowledge of the past, present, and future.

Nemesis: the goddess of vengeance who brings retribution on those who have sinned; the agent of retribution; an invincible rival in a contest or battle; or a necessary or inevitable consequence.

Nephilim: Another name for the Annunaki, ancient astronauts posited by Zecheriah Sitchin based on his interpretation of ancient Sumerian texts.

Nessie: See Loch Ness Monster.

Nursery Rhyme: Cute doggerel or poems supposedly written for the amusement of children. Much Pagan lore was hidden in these ditties during the years of witch persecutions.

New Age: The mixing of metaphysical practices with a structured religion.

New Religion: Pagan term used in reference to Christianity.

NICAP: National Investigations Committee on Aerial Phenomenon. UFO Group that was the most powerful in its heyday. For much of its existence Major Donald Keyhoe led it.

NIDSci: See National Institute for Discovery Science.

O

Occult: Often relating to, or dealing with supernatural influences, agencies, or rituals that often refer to or use in practices: Satanism, Supernatural, Magickal Beliefs, or other Mystical Phenomena. Literal meaning is "hidden" and is broadly applied to a wide range of metaphysical topics, which lie outside the accepted realm of mainstream theologies.

Occultist: One who practices and or studies a variety of occult subjects.

Ogham: Celtic equivalent of the Teutonic runes. The ancient alphabet of the Celtic people.

Old Hag: A form of sleep paralysis in which an individual senses a presence in his bedroom, even on the bed or on top of him. Palmer, Raymond - Editor of Amazing Stories magazine in the 1940's & later of Fate Magazine. Some credit him with originating the extraterrestrial hypothesis for the origin of UFOs.

Old Ones: The A term which refers to all aspects of the Goddess and God.

Old Religion: A name for Paganism as it pre-dates Christianity by at least 20,000 years.

Ontological: The philosophical study of the nature of being, becoming, existence, or reality, as well as the basic categories of being and their relations.

Oracle: (Mythology) A prophet who is about to communicate with the gods and deceased to foretell the future. See Seeres.

Orbs: Assumed to be a sign of paranormal activity, but is nothing more than an optical anomaly consisting of dust, bugs, or other particulate matter, including moisture. **Real Orbs:** Misidentified ball plasma, or illuminated by any other light source.

Ouija Board: Also known as, a spirit board or talking board is a flat board marked with the letters of the alphabet, the numbers 0-9, the words "yes", "no", "hello" (occasionally), and "goodbye", along with various symbols and graphics. It uses a planchette (small heart-shaped piece of wood) or movable indicator to indicate the spirit's message by spelling it out on the board during a séance. Participants place their fingers on the planchette, and it is moved about the board to spell out words. "Ouija" has become a trademark that is often used generically to refer to any talking board. See Ideomotor Effect.

Out-of-body experience (OBE): A sensation or experience in which one self or spirit travels to a different location than their physical body.

P

Pagan/Neo-Pagan: (Belief) followers of Wicca and other magickal, shamanistic, and polytheistic Earth-based religions. Also used to refer to pre-Christian religious and magickal systems. Christianity considers all non-Christians to be pagan.

Paganing: When a baby presented to the circle to the Goddess, and God. Their given a craft name, which a boy will keep until about 13 and at a girl's first menses. At their Coming of Age celebration when they can choose their own. Pagans who are not Wiccans for a type of baptism.

Papoose Lake: Another dry lake near Groom Lake or Area 51. Papoose Lake is where Bob Lazar claims that alien craft are being tested. Also known as S-4

Papua, New Guinea: Anglican missionary Father William Booth Gill reported UFOs over Boianai, Papua, New Guinea in 1959.

Paranormal: A general term that designates experiences that lie outside "the range of normal experience or scientific explanation", or which indicate phenomena understood to be outside of science's current ability to explain or measure.

Paranormal Entity: Any being that modern science has not officially recorded or classified.

Paranormal Investigation: The practice of going to a location where accounts of paranormal activity have been reported and working to investigate, rationalize, and/or document those specific claims.

Paranormal Investigator: A person who investigate paranormal phenomena.

Paranormal Phenomena are distinct from certain hypothetical entities, coupled with observation and scientific methodology.

Paranthropology: Is the Anthropological approach to studying the Paranormal. See Anthropology.

Para-celeb: A person that chasing fame or has reached celebrity status, although only within the paranormal community.

Parapsychology: J.B. Rhine adopted the term in the 1930s as a replacement for the term psychical research. Parapsychologists study consciousness with respect to telepathy, precognition, clairvoyance, Psychokinesis, near-death experiences, reincarnation and apparitional experiences.

Para-tard: A person that believes everything at face value unable to lean, or take the time to learn.

Para-wood: Hollywood aspirations although only within the paranormal community.

Pareidolia: A psychological phenomenon involving a vague and random stimulus (often an image or sound) being perceived as significant. Common examples include seeing images of animals or faces in clouds, and hearing hidden messages on records played in reverse.

Pascagoula, Mississippi: Site of the abduction of Calvin Parker and Charles Hickson on October 11, 1973.

Pandora's Box: (Greek mythology) a box that Zeus gave to Pandora with instructions that she not open it; she gave in to her curiosity and opened it; all the miseries and evils flew out to afflict all humanity.

Pantheism: Belief in many deities who are really one because they are all merely aspects of the single creative life source. Paganism is pantheistic.

Pantheon: A collection or group of Gods and Goddesses in a particular religious or mythical structure.

Past-Life Regression: Act of using meditation or guided meditation to pass through the veil of linear time and perceive experiences encountered in a previous existence.

Passion-Over Ritual: Ritual observed when a loved one has dies.

Path Working: Using astral projection, bi-location, or dreamtime to accomplish a specific goal. Also called vision questing.

Patriarchal: Term used to apply to the world since the matrifocal clans that worshipped Goddesses were supplanted by codified religions that honor all-male deity's.

Peer Review: (Science) A group of colleague's and experts that professionally evaluate a body of work.

Pendulum: A divinatory device consisting of a string attached to a heavy object, such as a quartz crystal, root, or ring. The free end of the string is held in the hand, the elbows steadied against a flat surface, and a question is asked. The movement of the heavy object's swings determines the answer. It is a tool, which contacts the psychic mind. See Ideomotor Effect.

Pentacle: (Belief) A circle surrounding a five-pointed, upright star (pentagram). Worn as a symbol of a witch's beliefs. Many witches consider wearing it inverted to be blasphemy of their faith and is commonly associated with Satanism.

Pentagram: (Belief) The basic interlaces five-pointed star, visualized with one point up. It represents the five elements: Earth, Air, Fire, Water, and Spirit. It is a symbol of power and protection.

Persephone: (Mythology) the harvest-goddess Demeter, and queen of the underworld, and abducted by Hades, the god-king of the underworld. Another daughter of Zeus.

Perseus: (Mythology) a demigod, the Greek hero who killed the Gorgon Medusa, and claimed Andromeda, having rescued her from a sea monster sent by Poseidon. The first of the heroes of Greek mythology whose exploits in defeating various archaic monsters provided the founding myths of the Twelve Olympians.

Personal Power: (Witchcraft) The energy, which sustains our bodies. It originates within the Goddess and God. We first absorb it from our biological mother within the womb, and later from food, water, the Moon and Sun, and other natural objects.

Phantom Hitchhiker/Traveler: A phantom traveler is the ghost of a human or animal that haunts a specific roadway, route, or vehicle. The phantom hitchhiker, who requests a ride, then suddenly disappears from inside the vehicle, is the best-known type of phantom traveler legend.

Phantom Smell: (Paranormal) anomalous odors, with no definable source, that can be smelled by unaided normal human olfactory senses.

Phantom Sound: Anomalous sounds, with no definable source, that can be heard by unaided normal human auditory senses.

Phantom Touch: The anomalous sensation of being physically touched, despite no physical contact being made with a material being or object.

Phenomenology: Used in many different disciplines Psychology, Architecture, Archaeology, and Science to describe a body of knowledge that relates empirical observations of phenomena to each other.

Philadelphia Experiment: Purported 1943 experiment by the U.S. Navy at the Philadelphia Naval Yards in which the U.S.S. Eldridge was made invisible, with dire consequences for her crew.

Philosophy: The study of general and fundamental problems, such as those connected with reality, existence, knowledge, values, reason, mind, and language.

Phoenix Lights: A huge UFO flap occurred in and around Phoenix, Arizona, on the night of March 13, 1997.

Phonology: Study of linguistics the production of sounds that comprise in language. Also known as The Study or Articulatory Phonetics Human speech created by the vocal tract.

Physical Manifestation: Situation wherein a supernatural entity physically appears in a manner visible to unaided normal human visual senses.

Physical mediumship: A form of mediumship in which the spirit communicates using both the physical energies and consciousness of the medium.

Planchette: A palm-sized triangular platform, usually on wheels, that is used as a pointer during the operation of an Ouija board.

Plato: (428–347 BC) a mathematician, student of Socrates, writer of philosophical dialogues, and founder of the Academy in Athens, the first institution of higher learning in the Western world. Along with his mentor, Socrates, and his student, Aristotle, Plato helped to lay the foundations of Western philosophy and science.

Polarity: The concept of equal, opposite energies. The Eastern Yin Yang is a perfect example. Yin is cold; yang is hot. Other examples: Goddess/God, night/day, Moon/Sun, birth/death, dark/light, psychic mind/unconscious mind. Universal balance.

Poltergeist: A Poltergeist, which means noisy ghost in German, is not really a ghost at all. A form of Psychokinesis usually generated unconsciously by an adolescent, but may come from an adult with a troubled mind. A poltergeist manifests itself in the form of knocking noises, object movement and other physical forms.

Polytheism: Belief in the existence of many unrelated deities each with their own dominion and interests who have no spiritual or familial relationships to one another.

Poppets: Anthropomorphic dolls used to represent certain human beings in magick spells.

Portage County, Ohio: Site where police chased a UFO for forty-odd miles in 1966.

Possession: The idea that a departed spirit can possess a person's mind and soul.

Post mortem Communication: A message delivered to a living person from a deceased one, usually delivered via a medium.

Precognition: foreknowledge of an event, type of ESP; foreknowledge of a paranormal kind.

Premonition: A feeling or impression that something, usually dire in nature, is about to happen and about which no normal information is available.

Price, Harry (17 January 1881 – 29 March 1948) was a British psychic researcher and author, who gained public prominence for his investigations into psychical phenomena and his exposing of fake Spiritualists.

Projective Hand: The hand thought to be the point through which personal power is sent from the body. Normally the hand used for manual activities such as writing, dialing the phone, etc. It is also the hand in which tools such as the athame and wand are held.

Pseudologia fantastica: Is also called mythomania, compulsive lying or pathological lying, is a behavior of habitual or compulsive lying. See Psychiatry.

Pseudo-science: A methodology, belief, or practice that claimed to be scientific, or that is made to appear to be scientific, but which does not adhere to an appropriate scientific methodology, lacks supporting evidence or plausibility, or otherwise lacks scientific status.

PSI: A blanket term used to denote or describe paranormal events, processes and causes. The purported process of information transfer or energy transfer in extrasensory perception or Psychokinesis that is unexplained in terms of known physical or biological mechanisms.

PSI Phenomenon: Any event, which results from, or is an instance of, PSI.

Psychic: A person (also called a sensitive) who professes an ability to perceive information hidden from the normal senses through extrasensory perception, or said by others to have such abilities.

Psychical: A psychic person uses empathic feelings to tap into nonphysical forces.

Psychical Research: Parapsychology; this term is still in use in Great Britain.

Psychokinetic Activity: The anomalous event of inanimate physical objects moved without interacting with a material entity or other discernible mundane source that would cause movement.

Psycho-kinesis: The ability to unconsciously control objects with only the mind.

Psychic Mind: The subconscious or unconscious mind, in which we receive psychic impressions. It is at work when we sleep, dream, and meditate. It is our direct link with the Divine, and with the larger, nonphysical world around us.

Psychiatry: Is the medical specialty devoted to the study, diagnosis, treatment, and prevention of mental disorders, among which are affective, behavioral, cognitive and perceptual abnormalities.

Psychism: The act of being consciously psychic, in which the psychic mind and conscious mind are linked and working in harmony. Also known as psychic awareness.

Pyramid Energy: Refers to alleged supernatural or paranormal properties of the ancient Egyptian pyramids and objects of similar shape.

Q

Quabala: See Kabbalah.

ULTIMATE PARANORMAL GUIDE

R

Red Bluff, California: Site where California Highway Patrolmen saw a UFO in 1960.

Radio Voice Phenomenon (RVP): Receiving the voice of a deceased human being over a regular radio.

Randle, Kevin: Author of many UFO books, including The Truth about the UFO Crash at Roswell with Donald Schmitt.

Randi, James born Randall James Hamilton Zwinge August 7, 1928 is a Canadian-American stage magician and scientific skeptic best known for his challenges to paranormal claims and pseudoscience. Randi is the founder of the James Randi Educational Foundation (JREF).

Raps/Knocks: Noises, often tapping in response to a request by the researcher.

Rare Earth Hypothesis: Hypothesis that, since the combination of factors that contributed to the evolution of intelligence on Earth are rare in the cosmos, then so must intelligence life be rare in the cosmos.

Raudive, Dr. Konstantīns: Research anomalies voices recorded on Electronic Reel-To-Reel Tape first discovered by **Friedrich Jürgenson**. Later known as

Electronic Voice Phenomena (EVP) published his book Breakthrough in 1971. Also, see Jürgenson, Friedrich.

Raudive Voice Phenomena: See Electronic Voice Phenomena (EVP).

Receptive Hand: The hand through which energy is received into the body. The left hand in right-handed persons, the reverse for left-handed persons.

Random Event Generators: Paranormal devices that allege to communicate with the spirit world using algorithms with internal libraries that will say random words. Other devices link words to different frequencies. The Spirit boxes also known as a Ghost Box, Franks Box scans through AM radio frequencies picking up weaker stations along with stronger stations broadcasting News, Talk, and God talk radio shows participant(s) perceiving certain words as meaningful. See Pareidolia.

Rede: The Basic tenet of witchcraft. "Harm none, do what thou will."

Regression Hypnosis: The practice of trying to recover lost memories by hypnotizing a subject and taking them back in their minds to the time in question. The problems with it are that the hypnotist can unwittingly plant "memories" in the subject's mind, and hypnotized subjects sometimes invent (confabulate) memories in order to comply with a hypnotist's requests.

Reincarnation: The process of repeated incarnations in human form to allow evolution of the sexless, ageless soul.

Rendlesham Forest: Forest near Woodbridge, Suffolk, England. It was the site of a well-known UFO event on 27 December 1980. Also known as the Bentwaters-Woodbridge UFO event.

Residual Entity: A supernatural being that evidences no intelligence or will of its own, and simply acts out the same scene or pattern of behavior repeatedly until the pattern fades away.

Residual Haunt: It is nothing more than an echo of past events playing repeatedly until the pattern fades away.
Unlike an intelligent haunting, it does not directly involve a spiritual entity aware of the living world and interacting with or responding to it.

Rhine Research Center Institute for Parapsychology, named after its founder J. B. Rhine, is a parapsychology research unit that "aims to improve the human condition by creating a scientific understanding of those abilities and sensitivities that appear to transcend the ordinary limits of space and time.

Rhine, Dr. Joseph B. and Dr. Louisa joined Professor William McDougall at the newly founded Duke University in 1927, the field of investigation into psychic phenomena was known as psychical research. At that, time psychical research was mainly concerned with working with mediums in the search for evidence of an afterlife. Conducted Studies on ESP, Psychokinesis (PK), telepathy, and clairvoyance.

Ritual Ceremony: A specific form of movement, a manipulation of objects or inner processes designed to produce desired effects. In religion, ritual is geared toward union with the Divine. In magickal works, it produces a specific state of consciousness that allows the magician to move energy toward needed goals.

Ritual Consciousness: A specific, alternate state of awareness necessary to the successful practice of magick. This state is achieved with the use of visualization and ritual. The conscious mind becomes attuned with the psychic mind, a state in which the magician senses energies, gives them purpose, and releases them toward a specific goal. It is a heightening of senses, an expanded awareness of the nonphysical world, a linking with nature and with Deity.

Ritual Tools: General name for magickal tools used by a witch or magician. They vary by tradition and usually represent one of the elements.

River Styx: (Greek mythology) a river in Hades across which Charon carried dead souls.

Robertson Panel: Pursue a 1952 CIA-sponsored panel that recommended a policy of debunking UFOs.

Rosicrucian Order (Rosicrucianism) a philosophical secret society said to have been founded in late medieval Germany by Christian Rosenkreuz. It holds a doctrine or theology "built on esoteric truths of the ancient past", which, "concealed from the average man, provide insight into nature, the physical universe and the spiritual realm." The Rosy Cross symbolizes rosicrucianism.

Roswell Incident: In July 1947, a rancher named Mac Brazel found some odd, silvery debris on the ranch at which he worked. He took some of it into the county sheriff's office and the sheriff turned it over to the local Army Air Base. The Air Base sent Major Jesse Marcel, the base intelligence officer, out to investigate, and he collected a lot of debris, which he took back to the base. Mac **Brazel** was held for several days for questioning, and the Roswell Air Base information officer released a story to the press that said a "flying disc" had been captured. Major Marcel and the debris were flown to Carswell Air Base in Texas, where General Roger Ramey held a press conference at which he announced that the debris was only a weather balloon. Years later, before he died, Jesse Marcel claimed that the debris was not a weather balloon, but that it was something "not of this Earth." Several popular books were written that claimed that an alien craft had been recovered at Roswell and that the incident was covered up by the military. Finally, in 1995, the Air Force issued a statement that the debris was that of a top-secret Project Mogul balloon train and radar reflectors. The debate still rages.

Runes: A set of symbols used both in divination and magickal work. There are several types will different origins- Scandinavian, Norse, Germanic.

S

Sabbat: A witch's festival.

Sasquatch: (Cryptozoology) The term "sasquatch" is an anglicized derivative of the word "Sésquac", meaning "wild man". The original word, in the Stó:lõ dialect of the Halkomelem language is used by the Coast Salish Indians of the Fraser Valley and parts of Vancouver Island, British Columbia.

Satan (Devil): A fictional being created to define God as a benevolent and loving God while separating all the vengeful and evil acts in the world as the work of the Devil. Satan has many names depicted throughout many faiths. Lucifer known as (morning star) found in the King James Version of the New Testament of the Christian Bible as a fallen angel cast out of heaven the epitome of all that is Evil.

Satanism: A belief in the fictional being. Satan developed in the context of the Christian faith, as an ideological backlash to certain tenets promoted in Christianity. The character of Satan revered by Satanists, therefore, is mainly regarded as the prototypical anti-Christian figure.

Scientific Theory: A theory that explains scientific observations, "scientific theories must be falsifiable" A scientific theory differs from any form of theory, which is defined as:

> A tentative theory about the natural world; a concept that is not yet verified but that, if true, would explain certain facts or phenomena.

> A belief that can guide behavior; "The architect has a theory that more is less"; "They killed him, based on the theory that dead men tell no tales." Thus, any idea can be called a "theory," but a scientific theory is more narrowly defined as something that explains a natural phenomenon and provides testable predictions that can be "falsifiable" (i.e., "proven false").

Scourge: Small device made from leather or hemp that resembles a whip. Used in flagellation rites within some religious traditions.

Scrying: A method of divination. To gaze at or into an object (a quartz crystal sphere, a pool of water, reflections, a candle flame) to still the conscious mind in order to contact the psychic mind. Scrying allows the scryer to become aware of events prior to their actual occurrence, as well as to perceive past or present events through other than the five senses.

Sedona: a town in Arizona that has acquired a reputation for being a UFO "hotspot".

Séance: A séance is an attempt to communicate with spirits. The word came to be used specifically for a meeting of people who gathered to receive messages from spirits or to listen to a spirit mediums' discuss with, or relay messages from spirits. Like the Ouija Board, this works on the principle that the group's intentions are to contact spirits. The attendees cannot control what comes through, and sometimes doorways or portals can be opened that allow other spirits through. See Table Tipping.

Seeress: In religion, a prophet is an individual who is claimed to have been contacted by the supernatural or the divine, and to speak for them, serving as an intermediary with humanity, delivering this newfound knowledge from the supernatural entity to other people.

Sensitive: See Psychic.

SETI: Search for Extra-Terrestrial Intelligence. The search for life on other worlds by using radio telescopes to listen for possible radio signals from space.

Shadow: Often refers to a remnant, of either a person or a thing, or literal or figurative meaning regarding partial darkness. See Apparition.

Shag Harbour: A harbor and town on the east coast of Nova Scotia where, in 1967, an unknown "something" fell from the sky into the harbour.

Shaman: A man or woman who has obtained knowledge of the subtler dimensions of the Earth, usually through periods of alternate states of consciousness. Various types of ritual allow the shaman to pierce the veil of the physical world and to experience the realm of energies. This knowledge lends the shaman the power to change his or her world through magick.

Shaitan Mazar: "Grave of the Devil". Location in Krygyzstan, in the former Soviet Union, where a UFO supposedly crashed. See also Return to Shaitan Mazar

Shamanism: The practice of shamans, usually ritualistic or magickal in nature, sometimes religious.

Shandera, Jaime: Producer of TV documentaries. Friend and associate of William L. Moore and Stanton Friedman. He was the individual to whom the roll of film containing the MJ-12 documents was delivered.

Shaver, Richard: Letter writer to Amazing Stories magazine. Claimed in letters to that magazine that events on Earth were being influenced by a race of evil underground dwelling creatures called deros. The letters were expanded and published by Editor Raymond Palmer as I Remember Lemuria and later became known as The Shaver Mystery. Shaver was once a mental patient and claimed he heard voices coming from his welding machine.

Shillelagh: Magickal tool corresponding to the staff in other traditions. Usually made from blackthorn wood.

Shriners: (Ancient Arabic Order of the Nobles of the Mystic Shrine) established in 1870, is an appendant body to Freemasonry.

Sight: Appalachian folklore term referring to psychic ability.

Sigil: Magically oriented seal, sign, glyph, or other device used in a magickal working. Ones you create yourself are the most effective. Sigils can be used on letters, packages, clothing, etc.

Sign, Project: The first official USAF investigation, which started in January 1948. Also known as Project Saucer. Probably the only honest Air Force effort to find out what UFOs were. The project ended in February 1949 when the goals of the Air Force regarding UFO investigations changed.

Simonton, Joe: Wisconsin farmer who claimed to have been given pancakes by UFO occupants in 1961.

Simple Feast: A ritual meal shared with the Goddess and God.

Simulacrum: Abstraction today is no longer that of the map, the double, the mirror or the concept. Simulation is no longer that of a territory, a referential being or a substance. It is the generation by models of a real without origin or reality: a hyper-real.

A slight, unreal, or superficial likeness or semblance.

Psychosomatic: It is a question of substituting the real as signs of the real.

Sitter: A person who sits with a medium at a séance or reading and receives a communication from a deceased individual through the medium.

Sitting: A gathering of individuals, usually led by a medium for receiving spirit communication with the dead. Also known as a "séance," a "spirit circle," or simply, a "circle."

Skeptibunker: A term sometimes used by UFO aficionados to lump both skeptics and debunkers together.

Skeptic: Expect facts and proof over beliefs. British spelling is Sceptic.

Skin-Walker: Native American legends, a skin-walker is a person with the supernatural ability to turn into any animal he or she desires.

Skinwalker Ranch: 2750 S, Utah 84063 also known as Sherman Ranch 480-acre Uintah County had reports over its 50-year history of alleged paranormal, and UFO activity. **Own by Robert Bigelow, and National Institute for Discovery Science (NIDSci).**

Sky Father: Shamanistic in origin. It assigns deification to the sky as a male entity.

Skyclad: The act of celebrating or performing magickal works in the nude. Considered deeply spiritual, NOT sexual.

Sleep Paralysis: A sleep disorder in which an individual awakens to sense a presence in his bedroom, even on the bed or on top of him. The victim is unable to move, hence the name.

Snippy: An appaloosa pony whose real name was Lady. She became famous in 1967 as the first "official" animal mutilation case.

Society for Psychical Research: The SPR founded in 1882 in London. The first organization of its kind in the world, its stated purpose being "to approach these varied problems without prejudice or prepossession of any kind, and in the same spirit of exact and unimpassioned enquiry which has enabled science to solve so many problems, once not less obscure nor less hotly debated.

Socorro, New Mexico: Lonnie Zamora, a sergeant for the Socorro Police Department, witnessed a UFO landing on Friday, April 24, 1964 in Socorro. His sighting has never been adequately explained.

Solitary: Pagan who works and worships alone.

SOPHIA: University of Arizona Department of Psychology Research Program investigates claims of communication processes involving various spiritual levels, from deceased individuals, through guides and angels, to purported communication with a higher power or divinity. Its focus is on healing and life-enhancement.

South Haven Park, Long Island: Site of an alleged UFO crash in 1992.

Spectrum Analysis: Software that is used by sound engineers to measure the magnitude of an input signal by its frequency components represented in a graphic visualization.

Spectrological: The study of Ghosts.

Spell: A magickal ritual, usually non-religious in nature and often accompanied by spoken words. It should be clear, concise, focused and emotional. Need must be present.

Spiral: Symbol of coming into being.

Spirit world: The place spirits go after death of the human form.

Spirit: A discarnate being, essence or supernatural force of nature. While a ghost is a manifestation of a spirit that has existed in human form.

Spirit Photography: A spirit photograph captures the image of a ghost on film. Many spirit photographs are supposedly intended as a mere portrait of a living human being, but when the film is developed, an ethereal ghostly face or figure can be seen hovering near the subject.

Spirit Portal: An area allowing cross traffic between our world and the spirit world. A form of doorway, it sometimes occurs in the form of a vortex. See Vortex.

Spiritual Guide: A spirit that watches over a living person and that offers wisdom or guidance. Referred to by some as a guardian angel.

Spiritualism: A belief system that spirits of the dead can (and do) communicate with living humans in the material world. Usually this contact is made through an intermediary known as a medium.

Spitzbegen: Norwegian Island inside the Arctic Circle where a purported UFO crash occurred.

Spook Lights: Lights, which appear in the skies regularly in the same area. Examples are Marfa, Texas, Joplin, Missouri's Hornet Light, and North Carolina's Brown Mountain Light.

Spook Show: Also called a ghost show or spookeroo, a spook show was a magic show, most popular during the 1950s, that featured horror- and ghost-themed magic tricks. Often one or two horror movies were shown as part of the evening's entertainment.

Sprite: synonymous with ghost, though more often synonymous with elf or fairy or used to refer to an elflike person.

Staff: Ritual tool, which corresponds to the wand or athame.

Stang: Ritual tool from Pagan Rome, which resembles a two-pronged trident. Often-used in place of the wand or circle.

Stargate Project: was the umbrella code name of one of several sub-projects established by the U.S. Federal Government to investigate claims of psychic abilities. Begun in the early 1950's the CIA started extensive research into Behavioral engineering, during this research, experiments were done using various Hallucinogenic substances, findings during these experiments led to the formation of the Stargate

Project, which handled ESP research for The Federal Government.

Stigmata: Term used to refer to the marks which appear spontaneously on the surface of the body in imitation of the wounds believed to have been received by Jesus Christ at the Crucifixion; sometimes observed on the bodies of certain devout individuals, and may also be induced by auto-suggestion or under hypnosis.

Stockton, California Daily Mail: (UFOlogy) There was at least one case of attempted abduction reported in conjunction with the mystery airships of the late 19th century. In 1897: Shaw claimed that he and a friend were harassed by three tall, slender humanoids whose bodies were covered with a fine, downy hair. The beings tried to accost or kidnap Shaw and his friend, who were able to fight them-off.

Stone Tape Theory is a paranormal hypothesis that was proposed in the 1970s as a possible explanation for ghosts. It speculates that inanimate materials can absorb some form of energy from living beings; the hypothesis speculates that this 'recording' happens especially during moments of high tension, such as murder, or during intense moments of one's life. This stored energy can be released at any given moment, resulting in a display of the occurred activity. According to this hypothesis, ghosts are not spirits at all, but simply non-interactive recordings, similar to a movie. Thomas Charles was one of the first to promulgate the hypothesis of residual haunting.

Strieber, Whitley: Fiction writer and abductee. Author of several books about his abduction experiences, beginning with Communion.

Sturrock Panel: a panel of scientists, headed by Stanford's Peter Sturrock, who studied the available UFO evidence and deemed the study of UFOs to be worthy of formal scientific investigation.

Succubus: a female demon believed to have sexual intercourse with sleeping men.

Subconscious Mind: Part of the mind which functions below the levers we are able to access in the course of a normal working day. This area stores symbolic knowledge, dreams, the most minute details of every experience ever had by a person.

Subliminal: A mental process below the threshold of consciousness that is perceived by or affecting someone's mind without their being aware of it.

Summerland: The Pagan Land of the Dead.

Sundog: A "false sun" formed by the sun shining through a cloud of ice crystals.

Supernatural Entity: See Paranormal Entity.

Superior image: A type of mirage that causes an image to appear above the horizon.

Sympathetic Magick: Concept of likes attract. Most common way spells are worked.

ULTIMATE PARANORMAL GUIDE

T

Table Tipping: Also known as, "Table Turning "is another type of séance, in which participants sit around a table, place their hands on it, and wait for the table to levitate or wobble back and forth. The table was a means of communicating with the spirits, or show that the spirit is present in the room. This dates back to the Fox sisters and the birth of Spiritualism.

Taff, Dr. Barry E. who holds a doctorate in psychophysiology with a minor in biomedical engineering, is a world-renowned parapsychologist who worked out of UCLA's former Parapsychology Laboratory from 1969 through 1978 as a research associate. During his four-decade career, Dr. Taff has investigated more than 4,500 cases of ghosts, hauntings, poltergeists and conducted extensive studies in telepathy and precognition, eventually developing the initial protocols and methodologies for what was later termed "remote viewing". He also, was himself, investigated as a psychic subject, the results of which were published in Behavioral Neuropsychiatry, "A Laboratory Investigation of Telepathy: The Study of A Psychic", Vol. 6, Nos. 1-12, April-December 1974-January-March, 1975.

Talisman: An object charged with personal power to attract a specific force or energy to its bearer.

TAPS: The Atlantic Paranormal Society founded by Jason Hawes, and Grant Wilson. Featured on the SyFy-reality TV series ghost hunters a production of Pilgrim Films. See Ghost Hunters

Tarot Cards: Set of 78 cards, which feature pictures and symbols, used to conn the diviner with the collective unconscious.

Tarologist: One adept at the art of handling the Tarot.

Tectonic Strain Theory: The theory that UFOs are electromagnetic phenomena that are generated by tectonic stresses in the earth's crust.

Tehran, Iran: Site of a well-documented UFO sighting on 19 September 1976.

Telepathy: Communication using the mind as opposed to other senses.

Teleportation: A kind of paranormal transportation in which an object is moved from one distinct location to another, often through a solid object such as a wall.

Temperilli, Gian: Author, Paranormal Investigator and Co-Author of the Late Famed Psychic Peter James Book "Heaven Can You Hear Me." Along with his daughter Sophia Temperilli co-hosts "The Ghost Host" on LiveParanormal.com.

Tesla, Nikola (July 10, 1856 - January 7, 1943) Known as a Serbian scientist, he was Romanian his original family name was Draghici, replaced in time by the nickname of Tesla, after the craft passed within the family, the carpenter (teslari). Arguably one of the greatest minds of the 20th century. Scientific achievements; Rotating Magnetic Field (1882), AC Motor (1883), Tesla coil (1890), Radio (1897), registering hundreds of patents.

> "The day science begins to study non-physical phenomena; it will make more progress in one decade than in all the previous centuries of its existence." ~ Nikola Tesla

Thomas Charles Lethbridge was one of the first to promulgate the hypothesis of residual haunting. Lethbridge did so in books such as Ghost and Ghoul, written in 1961. The subject was explored in Peter Sasdy's 1972-television play, The Stone Tape, written by Nigel Kneale. The popularity of the program has led to residual haunting become known colloquially as the "Stone Tape theory."

Threefold Law: Karmic principle that energy that is released, returned three times over.

Tommy Knockers: (Paranormal) the spirits of departed miners that help miners find ore. They also knock on the walls of the mines right before a cave-in. When you hear a Tommy Knocker knocking, it is best to depart the area right quick. They have saved the life of many a miner who has been in a danger

Traditional Haunting: See Intelligent Haunting

Tradition: Branch of paganism followed by any individual Pagan or coven.

Trance: A state of dissociation in which the individual is oblivious to their situation and surroundings, and in which various forms of automatism may be expressed; usually exhibited under hypnotic, mediumistic or shamanistic conditions

Trance Mediumship: A form of mediumship in which the medium shares his/her energy with a spirit through the use of a trance.

Trilithon: A stone arch made from two upright slabs with one lying atop these. They are featured in Stonehenge.

Trindade Island: a Brazilian island where, in 1958, a photographer on board a Brazilian Navy scientific research ship snapped several photos of a UFO.

Triple Goddess: One Goddess in all of her three aspects: Maiden, Mother, Crone.

Tsoukalos, Giorgio A. Is a Swiss-born (March 14, 1978) Greek writer, director, television personality, and proponent of the idea that ancient astronauts interacted with ancient humans. A 1998 graduate of Ithaca College in Ithaca, New York, with a bachelor's degree in sports information and communication.

Tully, Queensland, Australia: The first "crop circle" appeared in Horseshoe Lagoon near here in 1966. Twinkle, Project: A project to study the green fireballs seen in New Mexico in 1948 & 1949. The project was not adequately funded, and never produced any results.

U

USAF: United States Air Force.

UFO: See Unidentified Flying Object.

UFO group: Any organization whose main purpose is the study of UFO reports.

UFOlogist: A UFO investigator or researcher. A person whom studies UFO reports.

UFOlogy: The study of UFO phenomena.

Unidentified Flying Object: It does not necessarily mean an alien craft, although often used that way. An unknown object in the sky, called UFO.

Unidentified Submerged Objects (USOs): Are the lesser-known marine counterpart to UFOs. Like UFO reports, most USO sightings are either mundane, or impossible to verify. When a more traditional "flying saucer" decides to take a dive or rises from beneath the waves, called USO.

University of Colorado UFO Project: See Condon Report.

V

Valentich, Frederick: He and his Cessna 182 disappeared over the Bass Straits between Australia and Tasmania. Just before radio contact was lost, he reported that an unidentified aircraft was following his plane.

Vallee, Jacques: Author of several UFO books including Challenge to Science, Passport to Magonia, and Revelations

Varginha, Brazil: City in Brazil where, in 1996, aliens were supposedly captured or alien bodies recovered.

Variable Specific Impulse Magnetoplasma Rocket (VASIMR): VX-200 plasma engine is the next-generation plasma rocket being developed by former NASA astronaut Franklin Chang Diaz.

VERITAS: University of Arizona Department of Psychology Research Program of the Laboratory for Advances in Consciousness and Health (formerly the Human Energy Systems Laboratory) in the Department of Psychology at the University of Arizona was created primarily to test the hypothesis that the consciousness (or personality or identity) of a person survives physical death.

Virgin: Youngest aspect of the Triple Goddess. Also known as the Maiden. Represented by the waxing moon, colors white and blue. Her Sabbats are Imbolc and Ostara.

Vision Quest: Using astral projection, bi-location, or dreamtime to accomplish a specific goal. Also called path working.

Visualization: The process of forming mental images. Magickal visualization consists of forming images of needed goals during ritual. It is also used to direct personal power and natural energies for various purposes during magick, including charging and forming of the magick circle.

Villas-Boas, Antonio: Brazilian farmer who claimed to have been taken on board a UFO, where a female alien seduced him.

Vimanas: Ancient Hindu writings describe flying craft called vimanas.

VLF: Very Low Frequency range between 3 to 30 Hz borders on DC as well as AC.

Vodou: A Haitian Creole word that formerly referred to only a small subset of Haitian rituals. It is descended from an Ayizo word referring to "mysterious forces or powers that govern the world and the lives of those who reside within it, but also a range of artistic forms that

function in conjunction with these vodun energies."
Vodou often referred to as a Haitian religion.

Voodoo: Has a penchant for magick associated with curses, poisons and zombies. See Vodou.

Vortex: A mass of air, water or energy that spins around very fast, creating a vacuum to pull objects into its empty center. See Spirit Portal.

ULTIMATE PARANORMAL GUIDE

W

Walk-in: An extraterrestrial soul that has been invited to take over a human body by the body's current inhabitant.

Walton, Travis: supposedly abducted by a UFO from Apache-Sitgreaves National Forest in 1975. A movie of the event was called Fire in the Sky

Wand: Ritual tool brought to the craft from ritual magick.

Wanderer: An extraterrestrial soul that has chosen to be born into a human body.

Warren, Edward "Ed" Miney (September 7, 1926, August 23, 2006) along with his wife Lorraine were paranormal investigators and authors associated with prominent cases of haunting such as the Amityville Horror. In 1952, the Warrens founded the New England Society for Psychic Research, the oldest ghost-hunting group in New England, and opened The Warrens' Occult Museum. Lorraine Rita Warren still actively pursues her and her deceased husband's passion for investigating the unknown.

Washington Nationals: In July 1952, many pilots and radar operators reported UFOs in the Washington D.C. area. Some were attributed to false radar blips caused by a temperature inversion. However, some of the radar sightings were corroborated by visual sightings. These were never explained.

Warlock: Antiquated term misused in reference to a male Witch. It means oath-breaker or Liar. Most Pagans, Witch's find the term offensive.

Web Weaving: Networking with other magickal people via conversation, writing, e-mail, to gather information, which will mutually assist each party.

Wheel of the Year: One full cycle of the seasonal year.

White Lady: (also known as the Mulher de Branco) is a type of female ghost reportedly seen in rural areas and associated with some local legend of tragedy. White Lady legends are found around the world. Common too many of them is the theme of losing or being betrayed by a husband or fiancé. They are often associated with an individual family line or said to be a harbinger of death similar to a banshee.

White Magick: has traditionally referred to the use of supernatural powers or magic for good and selfless purposes. With respect to the philosophy of left-hand path and right-hand path, white magic is the benevolent counterpart of malicious black magic. Because of its ties to traditional pagan nature worship, white magick often also referred to as "natural magic".

Wicca: A modern Pagan religion with spiritual roots in the earliest expressions of reverence for nature. Some major identifying motifs are reverence for both the Goddess and God; acceptance of reincarnation and magick; ritual observance of astronomical and agricultural phenomena; and the use of magickal circles for ritual purposes.

Wicce: Synonymous with Wicca. In some circles, Wicce is used for women while Wicca is used for men.

Widdershins: Counter-clockwise motion, usually used for negative magickal purposes, or for dispersing negative energies or conditions such as disease.

Wilson, Grant: co-founder see TAPS.

Witch: A practitioner of folk magick, particularly that kind relating to herbs, stones, colors, wells, rivers, etc. It is used by some Wiccans to describe themselves. This term has nothing to do with Satanism.

Witchcraft: The craft of the witch- magick, especially magick utilizing personal power in conjunction with the energies within stones, herbs, colors, and other natural objects. This belief system also has nothing to do with Satanism.

Witching hour: A term for the time of night when ghosts are the most active, usually placed at between midnight and 3am

Wurtsmith AFB, Michigan: U.S. Air Force base in Michigan. Site of unusual UFO events in October 1975.

X

Xeno: (Greek Mythology) Meaning "alien," "strange," or "different" first used by the ancient Greek poet Homer. Sophocles uses the vagueness of the word xenos in his tragedy Philoctetes, with Neoptolemus using the word exclusively for Philoctetes to indicate the uncertain relationship between the two characters.

Xenoglossy: The act of speaking in a language ostensibly unknown to the speaker. See glossolalia.

Y

Yeti: (Cryptozoology) An ape-like creature taller than an average human. The names Yeti are commonly used by the people indigenous to the region of Himalayan region of Nepal and Tibet. Believed to be folklore or a part of their history and mythology. The scientific community generally regards the Yeti as a legend, given the lack of conclusive evidence, but it remains one of the most famous creatures of cryptozoology.

Yeremenko, Russian Major General Vasily: A senior retired official of the Ministry of Defense, lieutenant general in reserve, PhD, a fellow of the Academy of Natural Sciences Alexey Savin said that in the late 1980's a group of researchers from the Expert Management Unit of General Staff managed to make contact with an alien civilization.

Yggdrasil: One of the best-known Tree of Life symbols. It unites all existence from the Underworld, to the Physical world.

ULTIMATE PARANORMAL GUIDE

Z

Zaffis, John: Is a paranormal researcher the nephew of Ed and Lorraine Warren based out of Connecticut. Starred in the SyFy paranormal reality TV series "Haunted Collector", and runs the Paranormal and Demonology Research Society of New England, which he founded in 1998.

Zener cards: ESP cards, named after psychologist Karl Zener, who apparently suggested the symbols used on the cards. (Circle, cross, square, star and wavy lines)

Zero Point Energy (Quantum Vacuum): Is the zero-point energy of all the fields in space, and is the lowest possible energy that a quantum mechanical physical system may have; it is the energy of its ground state. Developed in Germany by Albert Einstein and Otto Stern in 1913, as a corrective term added to a zero-grounded formula developed by Max Planck in 1900.

Zeus: (Mythology) the "Father of Gods and men" King of all the Gods ruler of Mount Olympus. Also, see Jupiter. He is the god of sky and thunder in Greek mythology.

Zombie: As fictional undead creatures, zombies regularly encountered in horror and fantasy themed works. In Haiti, in a pharmacological case where a living person could be turned into a zombie by two special powders introduced into the blood stream. African beliefs the zombie is a temporary spiritual entity. Feeding a zombie salt will make it return to the grave.

Zoologist: A specialist in the branch of biology dealing with animals.

Zoology: The branch of biology that studies animals and animal life.